Home Science

Objective Type Questions Ability Test

For
NET/SLET/JRF

Home Science

Objective Type Questions Ability Test

For
NET/SLET/JRF

Kiran Yadav
M.A., B.Ed., ADCA
Keenaram P.G. College, Sonbhadra, Uttar Pradesh, India

O S Shekhar Singh
Ph.D.(Pur), NET, MLIS, ADCA
Under NVS, New Delhi
at
JNV Mewat (Old Gurgaon), Haryana, India

ATLANTIC
PUBLISHERS & DISTRIBUTORS (P) LTD

Published by

ATLANTIC

PUBLISHERS & DISTRIBUTORS (P) LTD

7/22, Ansari Road, Darya Ganj, New Delhi-110002
Phones : +91-11-40775252, 40775214, 23273880, 23275880
Fax: +91-11-23285873
Web: www.atlanticbooks.com
E-mail: orders@atlanticbooks.com

Branch Office: Chennai
Phones : +91-44-48531784, 28291383
E-mail: chennai@atlanticbooks.com

Printed & bound in India by Atlantic Print Services

Dedicated to

Our loving parents

Preface

Home Science (HS) is an interdisciplinary field of knowledge which draws upon many disciplines such as chemistry, physics, physiology, biology, hygiene, economics, rural development, child development, sociology and family relations, community living, art, food and nutrition, fabric and apparel designing, clothing, textiles, human development, resource management and communication, extension and home management, among others. It is being taught in India and abroad at various levels leading up to Master's degree. It is one of the very important disciplines in the United Kingdom, United States of America, India and many other countries. Education in Home Science is offered at four levels—diploma, first degree, postgraduate, and pre-doctoral/doctoral levels. More than 370 universities in India impart teaching up to Master's degree level besides the provision of doctoral programmes. It has also been popular and useful as a professional subject.

University Grants Commission (UGC) has evolved a method of selection and appointment to the university by holding a National Eligibility Test (NET) for Assistant Professors in all the subjects and Assistant Librarian for the university libraries. No appointment is possible without NET which is compulsory for this post in all universities in India. This condition is also applicable to HS professionals, planning to occupy senior positions. Some state level universities also conduct similar examination, i.e. State Level Eligibility Test (SLET) which is recognized by the UGC and given equivalence to NET.

This test is held twice a year which universities conduct in June and December. Union Public Service Commission (UPSC) holds this test as and when vacancies occur.

The papers are held on the same day in two separate sessions. Paper I is compulsory for all. It is of 100 marks having 60 objective type questions (in place of 50 questions earlier) and the candidate will have to answer 50 questions of their choice in this paper. Paper II and Paper III correspond to knowledge at the postgraduate level. Paper II is of 50 objective questions (Matching type, Multiple choice type, True/False, Assertion-Reasoning type) carrying 100 marks. Duration of these papers is 1 hour 15 minutes each.

Papers III will be of 150 marks and will have 75 objective type questions (Matching type, Multiple choice type, True/ False, Assertion-Reason type). Thus, Paper II will be of 100 marks and Papers III of 150 marks.

Since it is a National Level Test, it is expected that the candidates possess comprehensive knowledge of the subject. All questions are objective type. Paper III is evaluated of only those candidates who obtain the minimum marks fixed by UGC in Paper I and II.

The book covers Paper II and Paper III only and it contains only objective type questions (Matching type, Multiple choice type, True/False, Assertion-Reason type) with answers given at the end. There are seven chapters in this book. It is strictly designed according to the syllabi prescribed for NET/SLET and JRF examinations conducted by UGC and state level universities. All topics mentioned in the syllabi have been covered comprehensively.

It is hoped that this book will be help those aspiring for M.Phil. and Ph.D. programme in Home Science and aspirants of lecturaship in colleges and universities in the subject of Home Science.

Kiran Yadav
O S Shekhar Singh

Acknowledgements

We express our sincere thanks and deep sense of gratitude to our respected teacher Prof (Dr) M.T.M. Khan, Professor and Head—DLIS, Galgotiyas University, Greater Noida, Uttar Pradesh.

We acknowledge with sincere thanks the encouragement and suggestions given to us by Dr Suryakant, University Librarian, Sampurnanand Sanskrit University, Varanasi, and Dr Krishna Nigam, Principal Shri Agrasen Kanya Autonomous P.G. College, Varanasi. We also gratefully acknowledge the help of the staff of Central Libraries of IGNOU, New Delhi, Banaras Hindu University, Varanasi and Jawaharlal Nehru University, New Delhi, for providing all sorts of facilities and information needed.

We are grateful to our parents Dr Banwari Singh, Smt. Rajkumari and Mr Pramod Kumar Yadav who provided constant encouragement and moral support to complete this work.

We are extremely thankful to Atlantic Publishers and Distributors (P) Ltd., New Delhi for taking keen interest in the publication of this book.

Kiran Yadav
O S Shekhar Singh

Contents

Chapter 1

General Questions

1. Home Science means—
   (a) Arts (b) Science
   (c) Arts and Science (d) None of these
2. Major fields of Home Science are:
   (a) 3 (b) 2
   (c) 6 (d) 5
3. A short woman should wear clothes with:
   (a) Vertical lines (b) Horizontal lines
   (c) Diagonal lines (d) Plain
4. In modern times, there is an increase in—
   (a) Nuclear family (b) Joint family
   (c) Both (a) and (b) (d) None of these
5. Duty of care means—
   (a) Accepting responsibility for other people's mistakes
   (b) Giving out advice and relevant accident forms to injured members
   (c) Having a working knowledge of rules
   (d) Accepting responsibility for health and safety in workplace
6. What causes hair loss?
   (a) Trauma (b) Diet
   (c) Hormones (d) All of the above

Answer

1. (c) 2. (d) 3. (a) 4. (a) 5. (d)
6. (d)

7. The heart's primary function is to pump blood to which two main areas are
   (a) Lungs and heart
   (b) Lungs and rest of body
   (c) Main arteries and the aorta
   (d) Capillaries and lungs
8. Honey is a
   (a) Protein (b) Carbohydrate
   (c) Fat (d) None of the above
9. Which of these would be the healthiest choice for a snack?
   (a) Cookies (b) Chips
   (c) Peanuts (d) None
10. Children who drank about three 12-ounce sodas daily for 10 weeks gained
   (a) one pound (b) five pounds
   (c) seven pounds (d) lost weight
11. What is Threonine?
   (a) A Mineral (b) Amino Acid
   (c) Vitamin C (d) None of these
12. Alzheimer's disease:
   (a) begins abruptly
   (b) progresses slowly
   (c) progresses in three stages
   (d) is present from birth, but the symptoms appear only after age 65
13. Dentists recommend that you brush your teeth
   (a) twice a day
   (b) after each and every meal
   (c) when you start getting a funny taste in your mouth
   (d) it's a personal preference and varies among people

Answer

7. (b) 8. (b) 9. (a) 10. (b) 11. (a)
12. (c) 13. (b)

14. How many calories does water contain?
    (a) 50 (b) 100
    (c) 200 (d) None of these
15. Which of the following puts your heart at risk?
    (a) Cigarette smoking
    (b) High blood pressure
    (c) High cholesterol levels
    (d) All of the above
16. How many servings of fruits and vegetables should you have every day?
    (a) 1-3 (b) 2-6
    (c) 5-9 (d) 10-12
17. Breast feeding is often blamed for:
    (a) lack of sleep (b) headaches
    (c) marriage problems (d) all the above
18. The only way to stop the spread of HIV infection is through
    (a) regular treatment of infected persons
    (b) isolation of infected persons
    (c) prevention
    (d) voiding direct contact with infected person
19. What is the definition of health?
    (a) The absence of disease or infirmity
    (b) A state of being easily quantifiable
    (c) A state of complete physical, mental and social well being
    (d) A state of being subjectively assessed by individuals
20. Bipolar neurons are nerve cells that have
    (a) a single dendrite at the end of the cell and single axon at the other
    (b) several axons and a single dendrite

Answer

14. (c) 15. (d) 16. (a) 17. (d) 18. (c)
19. (c)

(c) many dendrites and a single neuron
(d) a single branch which after leaving the cell body divides into two directions

21. What causes warts?
(a) Bacteria
(b) Virus
(c) Poor hygiene
(d) Toads

22. What is a blood clot?
(a) A blockage in a blood vessel
(b) Blood that has thickened into a soft clump
(c) An impurity in blood
(d) A scab

23. What is the most correct procedure for first aid documentation?
(a) Gather information from bystanders and record in patrol log book
(b) Record events as witnessed, signed by first aider and kept on file
(c) Check with patient as to cause of injury, ensure next of kin notified and verbally pass information onto ambulance/paramedics
(d) Record all events as stated by bystanders and ensure patient signs as correct record

24. What causes vertigo?
(a) Insufficient rest
(b) An inner-ear problem
(c) Poor diet
(d) Excessive weight

25. Symptoms of a fracture
(a) pain and tenderness
(b) possible bleeding at wound site
(c) deformity and swelling at wound site
(d) possible discolouration

Answer

20. (d) 21. (b) 22. (b) 23. (b) 24. (b)
25. (c)

26. Why do we dream?
    (a) To stimulate our brain during sleep
    (b) To fulfill wishes and desires
    (c) To maintain our memory function
    (d) No one knows for sure

27. UNICEF organization works for the welfare of—
    (a) Children
    (b) Old people
    (c) Patients
    (d) Pregnant women

28. Which statement is true?
    (a) You can stop chronic bad breath by simply changing your diet
    (b) Generally, at least 50 per cent of the population has bad breath at any given time
    (c) Sometimes, people may cough up little white particles from their tonsils. Though these particles smell bad, they don't necessarily cause bad breath nor do they indicate any major health problem
    (d) On average, the human mouth harbors approximately 100 different types of bacteria

29. What are the four components of physical fitness?
    (a) Mental acuity, muscular strength, physical dexterity and energy efficiency
    (b) Aerobic endurance, cardiovascular strength, muscle density, mental outlook
    (c) Cardio respiratory endurance, muscular strength, muscular endurance and flexibility
    (d) Low body fat, agility, muscular appearance and cardio capacity

30. What can lead to athlete's foot?
    (a) Poor hygiene
    (b) Wearing the same pair of shoes every day
    (c) Wearing socks made of synthetic fibers
    (d) All of the above

Answer

26. (d) 27. (a) 28. (c) 29. (d) 30. (c)

31. How often should your toothbrush be replaced?
    (a) Every eight to 10 weeks
    (b) Every three or four months
    (c) Every other month
    (d) Every month

32. Research on social learning has demonstrated that aggressive behaviours
    (a) are imitated only if people observe the aggressive model in person
    (b) can be encouraged by viewing models who are rewarded for aggressive behaviour
    (c) are influenced by modelling but attitudes and beliefs are not
    (d) are not affected by non-aggressive behaviour

33. You should exercise at least
    (a) Two days/week (b) Three days/week
    (c) Four days/week (d) Five days/week

34. What is derived demand?
    (a) The demand for health
    (b) The demand for health care
    (c) The demand expressed by a health professional
    (d) The demand motivated by a health professional

35. Who needs the most calcium?
    (a) 14-18 year olds (b) 19-50 year olds
    (c) Those 51 and over (d) All of the above

36. Which statement is false?
    (a) People who have anorexia nervosa chance of recovering from their eating disorder than those who suffer from bulimia
    (b) Black women are just as prone to develop eating disorders as white women

Answer

31. (b) 32. (b) 33. (b) 34. (d) 35. (a)

(c) Eating disorders such as anorexia and bulimia weaken the bones, the individual has no appetite
(d) Recent research has uncovered a new eating disorder known as "night-eating" syndrome, where the individual has no appetite during the day but gorges at night

37. Which of the following statements is true?
(a) A breast feeding mother has to be extremely careful about what she eats
(b) Women with small breasts make less milk than those with large breasts
(c) A mother who smokes is better not to breast feed
(d) None of the above

38. Smoking increases your susceptibility to which of the following?
(a) Flu, pneumonia, tuberculosis
(b) Arthritis, lupus
(c) Infertility, menstrual cramps, and irregular periods
(d) All of the above

39. Which statement is false?
(a) Liver disease claims more than 43,000 lives in the United States each year
(b) Infections are the No. 1 cause of cirrhosis, a chronic disease which damages liver tissue
(c) Hepatitis A, B and C are all caused by viruses
(d) People suffering from liver disease generally are restricted to a diet high in carbohydrates, moderate in fat, and low to moderate in protein

40. What is vertigo?
(a) Dizziness caused by standing up too quickly
(b) Periodic headaches often accompanied by nausea
(c) A whirling sensation or feeling that the room around you is moving
(d) The opposite of horizontal

Answer

36. (d) 37. (a) 38. (b) 39. (b) 40. (c)

41. How much water do experts reckon people should drink every day?
    (a) 1 liter (b) 2 liters
    (c) 3 liters (d) 10 liters

42. Which sex has twice the rate of hip fractures as the opposite sex?
    (a) Male (b) Female
    (c) Can't say (d) None of these

43. Oncology is the diagnosis and treatment of which disease?
    (a) Tuberculosis (b) Kidney Failure
    (c) Cancer (d) Aids

44. The tongue has more than
    (a) 2000 taste buds
    (b) 1000 taste buds
    (c) 8000 taste buds
    (d) More than 10,000 taste buds

45. HIV/AIDS is not transmitted by
    (a) blood transfusions
    (b) organ or tissue transplant
    (c) use of contaminated injection
    (d) sharing toilets or wasting facilities

46. What is lactic acid defined as?
    (a) The highest volume of oxygen a person can consume during exercise
    (b) A waste product of aerobic energy production
    (c) The physiological stress on the body during exercise
    (d) A waste product of anaerobic energy production

47. The importance of drinking water immediately after a reflexology treatment is to
    (a) calm the client (b) flush out the toxins
    (c) stop micturition (d) induce perspiration

Answer

41. (b) 42. (b) 43. (c) 44. (c) 45. (d)
46. (b) 47. (b)

48. Our culture believes that we should all be independent of others and the earlier the better. This leads to:
    (a) a belief in "self-soothing"
    (b) a belief that a very young baby is trying to manipulate and control you
    (c) a belief in "letting the baby cry it out"
    (d) all the above

49. Why is a positive birthing experience so important?
    (a) It will be less painful
    (b) You won't be in labour so long
    (c) It's not all that important
    (d) A bad birth experience can cause a mother to feel anger, resentment or depression for years

50. What is the name given to the process of development and change over the lifespan?
    (a) Phrenology (b) Evolution
    (c) Ontogeny (d) Neural plasticity

51. Which of the following is not one of the phases of attachment development?
    (a) Pre-attachment
    (b) Perceptual selecting
    (c) Attachment in the making
    (d) Goal-corrected partnership

52. A common symptom of high blood pressure is:
    (a) headache
    (b) dizziness
    (c) rapid heartbeat
    (d) all of the above

53. How much should you exercise everyday?
    (a) 10 minutes (b) 30 minutes
    (c) 60 minutes (d) 90 minutes

Answer

48. (d) 49. (d) 50. (c) 51. (d) 52. (d)
53. (b)

54. Cobalamin is more commonly known as:
    (a) Vitamin C (b) Vitamin B_{12}
    (c) Vitamin A (d) None of these

55. What is Oleuropein?
    (a) Glycoside found in green olive leaves
    (b) An olive
    (c) Scientific name of the Green Olive Tree
    (d) None of these

56. What percentage of Americans over the age of 35 has gum disease?
    (a) Less than 10 per cent
    (b) Approximately 25 per cent
    (c) Exactly 50 per cent
    (d) More than 75 per cent

57. Drug addiction is:
    (a) a moral problem; bad people use drugs
    (b) a sign of weak willpower
    (c) a lifestyle choice
    (d) a disease

58. How does one get a chronic disease?
    (a) From smoking
    (b) From eating too much
    (c) You catch it from your parents
    (d) All of the above

59. What is not a symptom of anorexia nervosa?
    (a) Cold intolerance
    (b) Increased susceptibility infection
    (c) Skeletal muscle atrophy
    (d) High blood pressure

Answer

54. (b) 55. (a) 56. (d) 57. (d) 58. (d)
59. (d)

60. Angina occurs when
    (a) you're having a heart attack
    (b) not enough oxygen is reaching your heart muscle
    (c) you eat too much of that cheesy stuff on your nachos
    (d) there's air in between the heart spaces
61. A myocardial infarction is:
    (a) explosive gas
    (b) coronary heart failure
    (c) a heart attack
    (d) something that happens on the TV drama, ER
62. Why is there so much talk about antioxidants?
    (a) They may create free radicals
    (b) They may be effective in fighting obesity
    (c) They may reduce the risk of aging-related diseases
    (d) They may build muscle strength and endurance
63. How do we check for breathing?
    (a) Look, touch, feel
    (b) Look, listen, feel
    (c) Listen, look, touch
    (d) Touch, talk and listen
64. HIV/AIDS is:
    (a) one of the greatest challenges facing the world in the 21st century
    (b) an emergency of an unprecedented nature
    (c) a global disaster and threat to the world population
    (d) all of the above
65. What is the correct treatment for a nose bleed?
    (a) Stand, patient up, tilt patients head backwards, apply cold compress to forehead
    (b) Lay patient down in recovery position, apply soft bandage to nose

Answer

60. (b) 61. (b) 62. (c) 63. (b) 64. (d)

(c) Lay patient on back, elevate knees, reassure patient
(d) Sit patient down, tilt head forward, squeeze soft part of nostrils

66. Which statement is false?
(a) Vertigo can occur in children as young as 18 months
(b) Vertigo attacks may last anywhere from a few minutes to several days
(c) Vertigo can be very uncomfortable, but never life-threatening
(d) Benign positional vertigo is common among older people

67. What is a blood clot?
(a) A blockage in a blood vessel
(b) Blood that has thickened into a soft clump
(c) An impurity in blood
(d) A scab

68. The mobile parts of the spinal column are:
(a) Coccyx and sacrum (b) Vertebrae
(c) Thoracic and lumbar (d) Ligaments

69. An adult heavy worker male requires .... calories per day.
(a) 2000 (b) 2875
(c) 3800 (d) 1900

70. What happens in dextrinization?
(a) Coagulation (b) Gel formation
(c) Denaturation (d) None of these

71. Cotton clothes are made from:
(a) Sheep (b) Cotton tree
(c) Chemicals (d) Silk worms

72. Teething in babies start at the age of—
(a) 1 month (b) 3 months
(c) 6 months (d) 10 months

Answer

65. (d) 66. (a) 67. (b) 68. (b) 69. (c)
70. (c) 71. (b) 72. (c)

73. For home saving, following is the best option
    (a) Post office (b) Banks
    (c) Both (a) and (b) (d) Private agency

74. We should consume less of this if suffering from peptic ulcer
    (a) Spices (b) Fibrous food
    (c) Both (a) and (b) (d) None of these

75. The universal recipient blood group is:
    (a) A (b) B
    (c) AB (d) O

76. Which one of the following is not a tool of time management?
    (a) Peak load (b) Work curve
    (c) Rest period (d) Fatigue

77. The full name of O.R.S. is:
    (a) Oral Revolution Salt
    (b) Oral Rehydration Salt
    (c) Oral Rejection Salt
    (d) Oral Rated Salt

78. The first yellow milk that comes out of breast of mother is:
    (a) Serum (b) Cholesterol
    (c) Colostrum (d) Sterol

79. Which sentence is true?
    (a) Gout is more common in less developed countries than in the United States
    (b) Surgery is not a treatment for gout
    (c) Sometimes gout produces lumps under the skin around the ear
    (d) Eating dark-coloured berries or cherries will often trigger a gout attack

Answer

73. (c) 74. (c) 75. (c) 76. (d) 77. (b)
78. (c) 79. (a)

80. What is not a risk factor of colon cancer?
    (a) High calcium intake
    (b) Smoking
    (c) High-fat diet
    (d) Sedentary lifestyle

81. Which statement is true?
    (a) The faecal occult blood test is a colon cancer screening method used to detect the presence of abnormal cell development in faeces
    (b) Stools the thickness of pencils are a symptom of colon cancer
    (c) The common treatment for colon cancer is a permanent colostomy, where the entire lower colon is removed and a special bag is worn outside the body to collect waste
    (d) The American Cancer Society recommends that men start regular screening for colon cancer at age 50 and women at age 55

82. Which is a home remedy for heartburn?
    (a) Swallowing a tea spoon of yellow mustard
    (b) Sleeping without a pillow
    (c) Drinking milk
    (d) Eating peppermint candy

83. Which sentence is true?
    (a) You could never drink too much water
    (b) Athletes should choose sports drink over plain water to keep hydrated
    (c) If your urine is dark yellow, you probably need to drink more water
    (d) Water that's been frozen has lost essential hydration molecules

84. Without a tongue, what couldn't you do?
    (a) Chew, talk, taste, burp
    (b) Sing, talk, kiss, taste
    (c) Chew, taste, talk, swallow
    (d) Talk, swallow, smell, keep teeth clean

Answer

80. (a) 81. (c) 82. (c) 83. (c) 84. (b)

85. What is a hernia?
   (a) A non-cancerous, abnormal growth on the upper abdomen or near the groin
   (b) A clump of fat that bulges out from the stomach lining
   (c) The protrusion of an organ through a tear or weakened area or into a different part of the body
   (d) An inflammation of the intestines that appears as a lump, usually in the abdomen

86. Which is not a tongue disorder?
   (a) Long tongue (b) Hairy tongue
   (c) Tongue-tie (d) Black tongue

87. Which type of headache commonly occurs in adolescents and adults of both sexes?
   (a) Migraine (b) Cluster headache
   (c) Tension headache (d) Unisex headache

88. Where do warts not commonly appear?
   (a) Under the fingernails (b) On the forehead
   (c) On the back (d) On the feet

89. Which of the following is not a part of environmental hygiene and keeping your place free from clutter or conditions that allow bacteria and vermin to thrive?
   (a) Follow correct storage and garbage removal procedures
   (b) Maintain and clean equipments at the highest standard of hygiene
   (c) Carry personal hygiene kits (bum bags) with gloves and mask
   (d) Wash your hands regularly

90. A la carte menu is used in:
   (a) Railway Catering (b) Mid-day meals
   (c) College Hostel (d) Office Canteen

Answer

85. (c) 86. (c) 87. (c) 88. (d) 89. (d)
90. (c)

91. The fact that the child is learning new words and their meanings, at very rapid pace, is expressed by:
    (a) Syntax (b) Pragmatics
    (c) Semantics (d) Phonology

92. The first university to start a degree programme in Home Science was
    (a) Madras University
    (b) Delhi University
    (c) MS University (Baroda)
    (d) Punjab University

93. Swarnjayanti Gram Swarojgar Yojana was launched in the year
    (a) 1993 (b) 1995
    (c) 1997 (d) 1999

94. **Assertion (A):** Time is the human resource.

    Reason (R): Time is the easiest to be measured but one of the most difficult to understand.
    (a) (A) is true but (R) is false
    (b) (A) is false but (R) is true
    (c) Both (A) and (R) are true
    (d) Both (A) and (R) are false

95. Identify the correct sequence:

    The steps in managing the home are:
    (i) Planning (ii) Supervision
    (iii) Controlling (iv) Evaluation

    Codes:
    (a) (i), (ii), (iii), (iv) (b) (i), (iii), (ii), (iv)
    (c) (ii), (i), (iii), (iv) (d) (ii), (iii), (i), (iv)

96. Write the sequence of programmes of rural development by the years of commencement

Answer

91. (d) 92. (d) 93. (d) 94. (c) 95. (b)

(i) National Rural Employment Programme
(ii) Food for Work Programme
(iii) Development of Women and Children in Rural Areas
(iv) Jawahar Gram Samridhi Yojana

Codes:

(a) (i), (ii), (iii), (iv) (b) (i), (iii), (ii), (iv)
(c) (ii), (i), (iii), (iv) (d) (ii), (iii), (i), (iv)

97. Match the items in List I with List II:

List I	List II
A. Shabnam	(i) Gujarat Embroidery
B. Laddu Jalebi	(ii) Jamdani
C. Taipchi	(iii) Chikankari
D. Pachhi Patti	(iv) Bandhni

Codes:	A	B	C	D
(a)	(ii)	(iv)	(iii)	(i)
(b)	(ii)	(i)	(iv)	(iii)
(c)	(iii)	(i)	(iv)	(ii)
(d)	(iii)	(ii)	(i)	(iv)

98. Match the colour in List I with category given in List II:

List I	List II
A. Red	(i) Neutral colour
B. Green	(ii) Primary colour
C. Violet	(iii) Binary colour
D. Grey	(iv) Tertiary colour

Codes:	A	B	C	D
(a)	(i)	(iv)	(iii)	(ii)
(b)	(ii)	(i)	(iv)	(iii)
(c)	(iii)	(i)	(iv)	(ii)
(d)	(ii)	(iii)	(iv)	(i)

Answer

96. (c) 97. (a) 98. (d)

99. Which protein is found in egg?
    (a) Casein (b) Albumin
    (c) Gluten (d) Myoglobin

100. A fixed curriculum for teaching is followed in:
    (a) Extension Education
    (b) Non-formal Education
    (c) Informal Education
    (d) Formal Education

101. Match the following authors with the concepts they have introduced:

	List I	List II
A.	Vygotsky	(i) PWRE
B.	Piaget	(ii) Zone of proximal development
C.	Spearman	(iii) General factor
D.	Montessori	(iv) Auto education

Codes:	A	B	C	D
(a)	(i)	(iv)	(iii)	(ii)
(b)	(ii)	(i)	(iii)	(iv)
(c)	(i)	(ii)	(iv)	(iii)
(d)	(iii)	(i)	(ii)	(iv)

102. Match the programmes of development in List I with the years of commencement in List II:

	List I	List II
A.	Council for Advancement of People's Action and Rural Technology	(i) 1971
B.	Crash Scheme for Rural Employment	(ii) 1999
C.	Jawahar Gram Samridhi Yojana	(iii) 1993
D.	Employment Assurance Scheme	(iv) 1986

Answer

99. (b) 100. (d) 101. (b)

Codes:	A	B	C	D
(a)	(iv)	(i)	(ii)	(iii)
(b)	(ii)	(i)	(iv)	(iii)
(c)	(i)	(ii)	(iv)	(iii)
(d)	(iii)	(i)	(ii)	(iv)

103. Who is the Father of Kindergarten?

(a) Pestalozzi (b) Rousseau
(c) Locke (d) Froebel

104. **Assertion (A):** Egg yolk is used for making mayonnaise.

Reason (R): Egg yolk serves as an emulsifying agent in preparation of mayonnaise.

(a) (A) is true but (R) is false
(b) (A) is false but (R) is true
(c) Both (A) and (R) are true
(d) Both (A) and (R) are false

105. Arrange the following teaching learning methods in order of learner's ability

(i) A video show (ii) Laboratory method
(iii) Demonstration (iv) Radio talk

Codes:

(a) (ii), (i), (iii), (iv) (b) (iv), (i), (iii), (ii)
(c) (i), (ii), (iii), (iv) (d) (ii), (iii), (i), (iv)

106. Major source of energy for the body is:

(a) Protein (b) Glucose
(c) Fat (d) All of the above

107. Tocopherol is:

(i) Anticaking (ii) Antioxidant
(iii) Antibiotic (iv) Vitamin

Answer

102. (a) 103. (d) 104. (d) 105. (b) 106. (c)

Codes:

(a) (ii) and (iv) are correct (b) (i) and (iii) are correct
(c) (iv) and (i) are correct (d) (iii) and (iv) are correct

108. **Assertion (A):** 73rd Constitutional Amendment 1992 give Constitutional Status to Panchayat Raj Institutions. The amendment also made provision of 33 per cent reservation for women.

Reason (R): This amendment has empowered women politically and has brought a sense of political responsibility by giving functional and financial autonomy to Panchayats.

(a) (A) is true but (R) is false
(b) (A) is false but (R) is true
(c) Both (A) and (R) are true and (R) is the correct explanation
(d) Both (A) and (R) are true and (R) is not correct explanation

109. Which of the following micro-organism cause food borne intoxication?

(i) Staphylococcus aureus
(ii) E. coli
(iii) clostridium botulinum
(iv) Listeria monocytogenes
(v) Salmonella

Codes:

(a) (i) and (ii) (b) (i) and (iii)
(c) (iii) and (iv) (d) (iv) and (v)

110. For a successful outcome of the nutrition programme for the community, state the sequential order of steps to be taken:

(i) Implementation
(ii) Mobilising resources

Answer

107. (a) 108. (c) 109. (b)

(iii) Monitoring and evaluation
(iv) Priorities problem
(v) Identify target
(vi) Setting objectives

Codes:

(a) (v), (iv), (vi), (ii), (i), (iii)
(b) (ii), (i), (iv), (iii), (v), (vi)
(c) (iii), (iv), (i), (ii), (vi), (v)
(d) (i), (iii), (ii), (iv), (v), (vi)

111. Home Science is a field of knowledge and service primarily concerned with:

(a) Empowering women
(b) Empowering women and children
(c) Strengthening society
(d) Strengthening family life

112. The term 'Therbligs' was given by:

(a) Prang (b) Mundell
(b) Gilbreth (d) Denmann W. Ross

Answer

110. (a) 111. (d) 112. (c)

Chapter 2

Food and Nutrition Science

1. Which of the following is not the way to make sure you meet the highest standards of personal hygiene?
   (a) Limit the jewellery that you wear
   (b) Long hair must be tied back
   (c) Clean your teeth regularly
   (d) Wash your hands regularly
2. Damage from lack of oxygen to the brain begins in:
   (a) Less than 4 minutes
   (b) 3 minutes
   (c) 1-2 minutes
   (d) More than 5 minutes
3. What is a symptom of a blood clot?
   (a) Muscle pain
   (b) Lack of pulse in the affected extremity
   (c) Bluish skin tone
   (d) All of the above
4. Which sentence is false?
   (a) Blood clots that form in the lower extremities rarely travel upward in the body
   (b) Blood clots often clear up on their own
   (c) Renal vein thrombosis, a condition in which a blood clot forms in the vein that drains the kidney, is more serious in children than in adults
   (d) Blood clots can lead to tissue death

Answer

1. (a)   2. (d)   3. (d)   4. (c)

5. Where is your liver?
   (a) On top of the stomach
   (b) Below the gall bladder
   (c) Near the rectum
   (d) Below the large intestines
6. What is the percentage of fats and oils that should be included in the normal diet?
   (a) 10-15% (b) 12-15%
   (c) 25-30% (d) 30-35%
7. Anhidrosis is:
   (a) too much sweating
   (b) the scientific word for sweating
   (c) too little sweating
   (d) none of the above
8. What is a symptom of hereditary patterned baldness?
   (a) Rapid hair loss
   (b) One or more patches of hair loss
   (c) Thinning hair
   (d) Breaking of hair shafts
9. Hyperhidrosis can lead to:
   (a) fungal nail infections (b) heat rash
   (c) jock itch (d) all of the above
10. What group has the most scalp hair?
    (a) Brunettes (b) Blondes
    (c) Redheads (d) Skinheads
11. What increases the risk of developing a hernia?
    (a) Excess weight (b) Smoking
    (c) Abdominal strain (d) All of the above
12. The effects of caffeine in just one 8-ounce cup of coffee can be dangerous for:

Answer

5. (b) 6. (a) 7. (c) 8. (c) 9. (d)
10. (a) 11. (d)

(a) people with high-blood pressure
(b) pregnant women
(c) students taking exam
(d) tired drivers

13. Which sentence is false?
    (a) Changes in eating habits and medications are effective treatment for some hernias
    (b) It is very uncommon for women to have hernias
    (c) Hernias that cause severe pain require immediate attention
    (d) Some hernias in babies will disappear on their own before the child turns into an adult.

14. Which sentence is false?
    (a) Caffeine is not a nutritional requirement
    (b) If you are trying to eliminate caffeine from your diet, you should do so gradually
    (c) Drinking a cup of coffee won't help an intoxicated person "sober up"
    (d) Instant coffee contains more caffeine than coffee that's brewed

15. Heartburn is an inflammation of the:
    (a) Stomach (b) Heart
    (c) Throat (d) Intestines

16. What is colon cancer?
    (a) A disease in which cancerous cells are found in the large bowel
    (b) A malignancy located in the rectum
    (c) The growth of one or more polyps in the colon
    (d) Excess cell growth in the small intestine

17. What are symptoms of the heartburn?
    (a) Chest pain (b) Hoarseness
    (c) Coughing (d) All of the above

Answer

12. (a) 13. (c) 14. (d) 15. (a) 16. (c)
17. (d)

18. How can food poisoning occur?
    (a) Eating hamburger that's pink in the centre
    (b) Eating unrefrigerated hard cooked eggs from an Easter egg hunt the day before
    (c) Eating reheated leftovers form a week ago
    (d) All of the above

19. What is not a risk factor of gout?
    (a) Excessive exercise
    (b) Eating red meat
    (c) Eating spinach
    (d) Heredity

20. Approximately how many quarts of blood does the adult human body contain?
    (a) 2
    (b) 5
    (c) 10
    (d) 15

21. Who are most susceptible to shingles?
    (a) Newborn infants
    (b) People who've received the chickenpox vaccine
    (c) People who've had chickenpox and are undergoing treatment for cancer or AIDS
    (d) Elderly people who've never had chickenpox

22. What is the maximum number of egg yolks that you should eat per week?
    (a) One
    (b) Two
    (c) Three
    (d) Four

23. Which disease is the leading cause of death among women?
    (a) Cardiovascular disease
    (b) Breast cancer
    (c) Colorectal cancer
    (d) Lung cancer

24. Orange juice has a lot of which vitamin?
    (a) A
    (b) B
    (c) C
    (d) D

Answer

18. (d) 19. (b) 20. (b) 21. (c) 22. (c)
23. (a) 24. (c)

25. What lifestyle factor aids in the treatment of eczema?
    (a) Increase essential fatty acids in your diet
    (b) Take Vitamin K
    (c) Do more exercise
    (d) None of these

26. When is the World Diabetes Day observed?
    (a) May 1st (b) November 14th
    (c) June 15th (d) December 1st

27. Next to bacterially caused gum disease the most common cause of gum disease is:
    (a) accidents such as football injuries, car crashes, falls
    (b) self-inflicted brushing trauma
    (c) eating hot and spicy foods
    (d) smoking cigarettes and chewing tobacco

28. What do bones store that can be reabsorbed by the body if needed?
    (a) Fat (b) Minerals
    (c) Both (a) and (b) (d) Oxygen

29. What is the shelf life of honey?
    (a) A couple of weeks
    (b) It needs to be refrigerated after one year
    (c) No more than five years
    (d) Thousands of years

30. Which of the following is not true about skeletal muscles?
    (a) They usually link two bones across a joint
    (b) They are voluntary muscles, responsible for movement
    (c) When they contract, they get larger and longer
    (d) They appear "striped" and so are also called striated muscles

31. The heart's primary function is to pump blood to which two main areas are

Answer

25. (b) 26. (b) 27. (d) 28. (c) 29. (d)
30. (a)

(a) Lungs and heart
(b) Lungs and rest of body
(c) Main arteries and the aorta
(d) Capillaries and lungs

32. Honey is a
(a) Protein
(b) Carbohydrate
(c) Fat
(d) None of the above

33. What symptom of Alzheimer's is present from beginning to end?
(a) Argumentativeness
(b) Poor hygiene
(c) Wandering
(d) Loss of interest and initiative

34. What percentage of our daily calorie intake (energy) should come from carbohydrates?
(a) 50 per cent
(b) 80 per cent
(c) 100 per cent
(d) Zero per cent

35. What is the best kind of fish for your heart?
(a) Walleye
(b) Northern
(c) Goldfish
(d) Salmon

36. Which of the following can damage and we don't know any more about the baby's growing brain?
(a) Teratogens
(b) Certain diseases during pregnancy
(c) Early child abuse and neglect
(d) All of the above

37. The most appropriate fluid to give to a conscious patient suffering from hypothermia is:
(a) Cool freshwater
(b) Sweet carbonated drinks

Answer

31. (b) 32. (b) 33. (d) 34. (a) 35. (d)
36. (d)

(c) A small amount of alcohol
(d) Warm, sweet drinks

38. The treatment of a sprain
(a) Immobilize
(b) Stretch the muscle
(c) Apply ice, elevation and compression
(d) Apply heat, elevation and compression

39. Which of these dark-green leafy vegetables is not a good source of calcium?
(a) Spinach (b) Broccoli
(c) Kale (d) Mustard

40. What are antioxidants?
(a) Minerals (b) Phytochemicals
(c) Pollutants (d) Enzymes

41. What's the serving size for raw, leafy vegetables?
(a) 4 handfuls (b) 6 cups
(c) 1 cup (d) 12 leaves

42. How does your body use calcium?
(a) In building and maintaining strong bones
(b) In maintaining heart function
(c) In digestion
(d) Both (a) and (b)

43. Who said a baby crib is the breeding ground for many of the mental health and social ills in Western societies?
(a) The creators of "Marlboro man" ads
(b) Dr. Michael Commons, Harvard Medical School
(c) Oprah Winfrey
(d) Stone Cold Steve Austin

44. What are the advantages of having a baby without medication?

Answer

37. (d) 38. (c) 39. (a) 40. (a) 41. (a)
42. (d) 43. (b)

(a) Babies born without drugs are more active and alert
(b) Right after birth the mother can comfort, stroke and gaze at her baby
(c) Breast feeding is more easily established
(d) All of the above

45. Protein can be found in which food?
(a) Broccoli (b) Meat
(c) Pie (d) Pizza

46. Which of these foods contains the most calcium?
(a) A cup of skim milk
(b) A cup of 2% yogurt
(c) A cup of 2% ice cream
(d) A cup of 2% cottage cheese

47. How much calcium do we need to be healthy?
(a) 100 mg per day
(b) 400 mg per day
(c) 700 mg per day
(d) No fixed amount

48. How often should you eat fish, according to experts?
(a) Once a week (b) Twice a week
(c) Every day (d) Once a month

49. Oncology is the diagnosis and treatment of which disease?
(a) Tuberculosis (b) Kidney Failure
(c) Cancer (d) Aids

50. What is the human trachea also called?
(a) Windpipe (b) Lungs
(c) Small Intestine (d) Large Intestine

51. Bread, cereal, potatoes and spaghetti are all good sources of what?
(a) Carbohydrates (b) Fluoride
(c) Sugar (d) Vitamins

Answer

44. (d) 45. (b) 46. (d) 47. (d) 48. (c)
49. (c) 50. (a) 51. (a)

52. Which of these would be the healthiest choice for a snack?
    (a) Cookies (b) Chips
    (c) Peanuts (d) None
53. All women should include what in their diets to help prevent osteoporosis?
    (a) More calcium, either from dietary sources or from calcium supplements Vitamin D
    (b) High sodium foods
    (c) More calcium and Vitamin D
    (d) None of these
54. What is lactic acid defined as?
    (a) The highest volume of oxygen a person can consume during exercise
    (b) A waste product of aerobic energy production
    (c) The physiological stress on the body during exercise
    (d) A waste product of anaerobic energy production
55. Too much sodium in your diet can cause
    (a) increased blood pressure
    (b) increased blood volume causing your heart to work harder
    (c) retention of fluid
    (d) all of the above
56. What is the largest number of cups of caffeinated coffee that should be consumed per day?
    (a) One cup (b) Two cups
    (c) Three cups (d) Four cups
57. What is the most important drink to have everyday?
    (a) Milk (b) Water
    (c) Gatorade (d) Tea
58. Why are green vegetables so important?

Answer

52. (a) 53. (c) 54. (b) 55. (d) 56. (b)
57. (a)

(a) They look good in salads
(b) They keep your teeth shiny
(c) They have lots of vitamins and minerals
(d) None of these

59. You should always try to avoid too much of which food?
(a) Peanuts (b) Candy
(c) Apples (d) None

60. How many eggs does it take to fulfill one serving of meat?
(a) 1 (b) 1-2
(c) 2-3 (d) 4-5

61. Why should you eat many different types of fruits?
(a) They make a fruit salad in your stomach
(b) Eating the same fruits gets boring
(c) Each contain certain nutrients that are important
(d) None of these

62. Sugar contributes to tooth decay because
(a) sugar directly attacks tooth enamel
(b) sugar combines with salivary proteins to create a harden layer of film over tooth surfaces
(c) sugar is converted by bacteria into acid which attacks tooth surfaces
(d) sugar mechanically abrades tooth surfaces

63. A calorie is:
(a) the amount of energy needed to raise the temperature of one gram of water by one degree celsius
(b) a nutrient
(c) a point system devised by dietician to describe the amount of fats in a particular food
(d) None of these

64. One pound equals how many calories?

Answer

58. (c) 59. (b) 60. (c) 61. (c) 62. (c)
63. (a)

(a) 1,000 (b) 150
(c) 3,500 (d) 1,250

65. Fats, carbohydrates and proteins contain how many calories per gram?
(a) 50, 20 and 10 (b) 14, 19 and 30
(c) 9, 4 and 4 (d) None of the above

66. What are the major types of eating disorders?
(a) Anorexia nervosa and bulimia nervosa
(b) Anorexia nervosa, bulimia nervosa and binge eating
(c) Anorexia nervosa, bulimia nervosa, binge eating and obesity
(d) Anorexia nervosa, bulimia nervosa, binge eating, obesity and starvation

67. In a study of lean, active adolescents and obese, sedentary kids, which group consumed the most calories?
(a) The lean, active kids
(b) The obese, sedentary kids
(c) All of these combined
(d) None of these

68. The recommended serving size of cooked cereal, rice or pasta is:
(a) 1-1/2 cups (b) 1/2 cup
(c) 12 ounces (d) 2 cups

69. What's the recommended serving size of fruit?
(a) 2 cups
(b) 10 ounces
(c) 1 piece
(d) It varies, depending on the type and form

70. The recommended serving size of milk, yogurt or cheese is:

Answer

64. (c) 65. (c) 66. (d) 67. (a) 68. (a)
69. (d)

(a) 2/3 cup for each
(b) 1 cup low-fat or nonfat milk or yogurt; 1-1/2 ounces low-fat natural cheese
(c) 6 ounces for each
(d) 3/4 cup low-fat or nonfat milk or yogurt; 2 ounces low-fat natural cheese

71. Why are proteins important?
(a) They improve mental clarity
(b) They build enzymes, muscles, tissues, hormones and red blood cells
(c) They provide the body with energy
(d) They build muscle strength and endurance

72. Which of the foods or combinations of foods provide good quality protein?
(a) Sashimi (raw fish) and steak
(b) Eggs
(c) Beans and brown rice
(d) All of the above

73. Which of these foods contain no protein?
(a) Butter (b) Rice
(c) Peanut butter (d) Kale

74. Which is not essential in a balanced diet normally?
(a) Fruits and vegetables (b) Salads
(c) Pulses (d) Tea

75. Proportion of rice and dal in the dish of Dosa is?
(a) 3 : 4 (b) 1 : 2
(c) 3 : 1 (d) 2 : 2

76. Haemoglobin is a ..... type of protein.
(a) Simple (b) Conjugated
(c) Derived (d) Animal protein

Answer

70. (d) 71. (b) 72. (d) 73. (d) 74. (d)
75. (c) 76. (b)

77. Egg contains all the nutrients except:
    (a) Avidin (b) Riboflavin
    (c) Carbohydrates (d) Biotin

78. Which cooking oil has the highest amount of essential fatty acids?
    (a) Groundnut oil (b) Coconut oil
    (c) Sunflower oil (d) Castor oil

79. Total protein synthesized during pregnancy is:
    (a) 900 gm (b) 700 gm
    (c) 1200 gm (d) 1500 gm

80. In hepatic coma the diet given is:
    (a) High protein
    (b) Low protein
    (c) High carbohydrate
    (d) High protein, high calorie

81. The basic food items are like "Atta, Suji, Milk, Edible oils" are standardized and marketed under the marks?
    (a) AGMARK (b) ISI
    (c) FPO (d) BIS

82. Which is the best method to cook vegetables?
    (a) Frying (b) Baking
    (c) Boiling (d) Steaming

83. Ascorbic acid is the name of vitamin?
    (a) A (b) B
    (c) C (d) D

84. For home saving, following is the best option:
    (a) Post office (b) Banks
    (c) Both (a) and (b) (d) Private agency

Answer

77. (c) 78. (c) 79. (b) 80. (b) 81. (a)
82. (d) 83. (c) 84. (c)

85. Riboflavin vitamin is not found in:

(a) Fish (b) Apple
(c) Yeast (d) Milk powder

86. Which of the following is not caused due to deficiency of Vitamin A?

(a) Night blindness (b) Conjuctivitis
(c) Keratomalacia (d) Ketosis

87. Which sentence is true?

(a) Game meat usually contains little bacteria because wild animals have a more natural diet
(b) It's always safe to eat food that doesn't taste, bad, has no offending odour, or isn't discoloured
(c) Cream, custard or meringue pies and foods with custard fillings should be kept cool until served
(d) Freezing will kill bacteria in food

88. Food cooked in a microwave oven must reach at least:

(a) 145°F (b) 155°F
(c) 165°F (d) 180°F

89. Which group is most vulnerable to life-threatening illnesses due to food poisoning?

(a) Young children (b) The elderly
(c) Pregnant women (d) All of the above

90. Hernias may occur in what parts of the body?

(a) Groin, upper thigh, near the navel, chest
(b) Throat, stomach, near the shoulder, pelvis
(c) Lower thigh, armpit, groin, buttocks
(d) Stomach, face, chest, knee

91. Calluses and corns are often a symptom of what?

(a) Ill-fitting shoes
(b) A particular style of walking

Answer

85. (d) 86. (b) 87. (c) 88. (c) 89. (d)
90. (c)

(c) A bony deformity
(d) All of the above

92. Richest source of Vitamin C is:
(a) Orange (b) Cabbage
(c) Amla (d) Sprouts

93. Micro-organisms can be rendered inactive:
(a) By boiling (b) By freezing
(c) By Dehydration (d) All of these

94. Nutritional Anaemia can be caused due to deficiency of:
(a) Iron (b) Folic acid and B_{12}
(c) Protein (d) All of these

95. Milk can be curdled by using:
(a) Whey water (b) Rennin
(c) Lemon juice (d) All of these

96. **Assertion (A):** Consumption of lythrus stivus causes lathyrism, a crippling disease.

Reason (R): Lythrus stivus contains a water soluble toxic alkaloid called BOAA.
(a) (A) is true but (R) is false
(b) (A) is false but (R) is true
(c) Both (A) and (R) are true
(d) Both (A) and (R) are false

97. **Assertion (A):** Egg yolk is used for making mayonnaise.

Reason (R): Egg yolk is added to give bright yellow colour to mayonnaise.
(a) (A) is true but (R) is false
(b) (A) is false but (R) is true
(c) Both (A) and (R) are true
(d) Both (A) and (R) are false

Answer

91. (d) 92. (c) 93. (d) 94. (d) 95. (d)
96. (c) 97. (a)

98. Arrange the following Vitamin A deficiency symptoms according to its manifestation in the disease.

(i) Bitot's spot (ii) Night blindness
(iii) Xcropthalmia (iv) Keratomalacia

Codes:

(a) (i), (ii), (iii), (iv) (b) (ii), (iii), (iv), (i)
(c) (ii), (i), (iii), (iv) (d) (ii), (iii), (i), (iv)

99. Arrange in sequence the phases of fat absorption:

(i) Emulsification (ii) Esterification
(iii) Mucosal uptake (iv) Chylomicron formation

Codes:

(a) (i), (ii), (iii), (iv) (b) (ii), (iii), (iv), (i)
(c) (i), (iii), (ii), (iv) (d) (ii), (iii), (i), (iv)

100. Match the following in List I (Additives) with List II (Foods):

List I	List II
A. Potassium Metabisulphite	(i) Grape Juice
B. Sodium Benzoate	(ii) Pineapple Juice
C. Acetic Acid	(iii) Jam
D. Pectin	(iv) Sauce

Codes:	A	B	C	D
(a)	(i)	(iv)	(iii)	(ii)
(b)	(ii)	(i)	(iv)	(iii)
(c)	(iv)	(iii)	(ii)	(i)
(d)	(iii)	(ii)	(i)	(iv)

101. Match the symptoms in List I with nutrients List II:

List I	List II
A. Dementia	(i) Iodine
B. Cretinism	(ii) Fat
C. Keratomalacia	(iii) Naicin
D. Hyperkerotosis	(iv) Vitamin A

Answer

98. (c) 99. (c) 100. (a)

Codes:	A	B	C	D
(a)	(i)	(iv)	(iii)	(ii)
(b)	(ii)	(i)	(iv)	(iii)
(c)	(iii)	(i)	(iv)	(ii)
(d)	(iii)	(ii)	(i)	(iv)

102. Match the items in List I with List II:

List I	List II
A. Bulimia	(i) Identity crisis
B. Alodescence	(ii) Eating disorder
C. Saccades	(iii) Seeing and hearing
D. Wernick's area	(iv) Eye movements

Codes:	A	B	C	D
(a)	(i)	(iv)	(iii)	(ii)
(b)	(ii)	(i)	(iv)	(iii)
(c)	(iii)	(i)	(iv)	(ii)
(d)	(iii)	(ii)	(i)	(iv)

103. Food spoilage can occur due to:
   (a) Growth of micro-organism
   (b) High temperature
   (c) Low temperature
   (d) Storage

104. Which of the following is an antioxidant?
   (a) β Carotene (b) Vitamin C
   (c) Selenium (d) All of these

105. Which of the following is an essential fatty acid?
   (a) Palmitic acid (b) Stearic acid
   (c) Linoleric acid (d) Oleic acid

106. Which protein is found in egg?
   (a) Casein (b) Albumin
   (c) Gluten (d) Myoglobin

Answer

101. (c) 102. (b) 103. (a) 104. (c) 105. (c)
106. (b)

107. Which one of the following is summated rating scale used to measure attitudes:

(a) Bogardus scale (b) Thurstone scale
(c) Likert's scale (d) Guttman's scale

108. **Assertion (A):** Before sundrying the vegetable should be blanched.

Reason (R): High temperature used in blanching kills certain micro-organisms but does not inactivate the enzymes.

(a) (A) is true but (R) is false
(b) (A) is false but (R) is true
(c) Both (A) and (R) are true
(d) Both (A) and (R) are false

109. Arrange the steps of cotton spinning system in the correct sequence:

(i) Drawing (ii) Carding
(iii) Combing (iv) Roving

Codes:

(a) (ii), (i), (iii), (iv) (b) (i), (iii), (ii), (iv)
(c) (i), (ii), (iii), (iv) (d) (ii), (iii), (i), (iv)

110. Match the adulterant in List I with foods in List II:

List I	**List II**
A. Pepper	(i) Papaya seed
B. Chilli powder	(ii) Brick
C. Turmeric	(iii) Cow dung
D. Corriander powder	(iv) Metalin yellow

Codes:	**A**	**B**	**C**	**D**
(a)	(i)	(iv)	(iii)	(ii)
(b)	(ii)	(i)	(iv)	(iii)
(c)	(i)	(ii)	(iv)	(iii)
(d)	(iii)	(ii)	(i)	(iv)

Answer

107. (c) 108. (c) 109. (a) 110. (c)

111. Match the items in List I with List II:

List I	List II
A. Geyser	(i) Condenser
B. Refrigerator	(ii) Choke
C. Cooking range	(iii) Gas Cylinder
D. Tube light	(iv) Thermostat

Codes:	A	B	C	D
(a)	(i)	(iv)	(iii)	(ii)
(b)	(ii)	(i)	(iv)	(iii)
(c)	(iv)	(i)	(iii)	(ii)
(d)	(iii)	(i)	(ii)	(iv)

112. Absorption of Iron requires the following nutrients in the diet:

(a) Vitamin C
(b) Zinc
(c) Iodine
(d) Fat

113. Which of the following is an ω-3 (omega 3) fatty acid?

(a) Linoleic acid
(b) α-Linolenic acid
(c) Arachadonic acid
(d) Oleic acid

114. Which is the major protein found in milk:

(a) Albumin
(b) Casein
(c) Myoglobin
(d) Gliadin

115. The supplementary nutrition provided to preschooler at ICDS should provide:

(a) 350 calories and 10 g protein
(b) 300 calories and 10 g protein
(c) 600 calories and 16 g protein
(d) 300 calories and 8 g protein

116. **Assertion (A):** High salt and low potassium intakes are a risk factor for developing hypertension.

Reason (R): Consuming plenty of fruits and vegetables are recommended for hypertension.

Answer

111. (c) 112. (a) 113. (b) 114. (b) 115. (b)

(a) (A) is true but (R) is partially correct
(b) (A) is false but (R) is true
(c) Both (A) and (R) are true
(d) Both (A) and (R) are false

117. **Assertion (A):** Both Vitamin A and fat are required for vision in the dark.

Reason (R): Fat helps in absorption of Vitamin A in the gut.

(a) (A) is true but (R) is false
(b) (A) is false but (R) is true
(c) Both (A) and (R) are true
(d) Both (A) and (R) are false

118. Give the correct sequence of steps involved in sugar cookery.

(i) Soft ball (ii) Hard crack
(iii) Carmel (iv) 2 thread
(v) Hard ball

Codes:

(a) (ii), (i), (iii), (iv), (v) (b) (iv), (i), (v), (ii), (iii)
(c) (ii), (i), (iii), (v), (iv) (d) (ii), (iii), (i), (iv), (v)

119. Give the correct sequence of foods in decreasing order of iron content:

(i) Liver (ii) Apple
(iii) Dates (iv) Wheat flour
(v) Lotus stem

Codes:

(a) (i), (ii), (iii), (iv), (v) (b) (iv), (i), (v), (ii), (iii)
(c) (ii), (i), (iii), (iv), (v) (d) (ii), (iii), (i), (iv), (v)

120. Give the correct sequence of appearance of symptoms of vitamin A deficiency:

(i) Bitot spots (ii) Conjunctival xerosis
(iii) Night blindness (iv) Keratomalacia

Answer

116. (a) 117. (b) 118. (b) 119. (c)

Codes:

(a) (i), (ii), (iii), (iv)   (b) (iv), (i), (iii), (ii)
(c) (ii), (i), (iii), (iv)   (d) (iii), (i), (iv), (ii)

121. Give the correct sequencing for processing a cotton fabric:
(a) Bleaching, designing, tentering, calendering
(b) Designing, bleaching, tentering, calendering
(c) Tentering, bleaching, designing, calendering
(d) Calendering, bleaching, designing, tentering

122. Match the colour of fruit and vegetable in List I with the pigment in List II:

List I	List II
A. Green	(i) Carotenoids
B. Deep yellow	(ii) Chlorophyll
C. White	(iii) Anthocyanin
D. Purple	(iv) Flavones

Codes:	A	B	C	D
(a)	(i)	(iv)	(iii)	(ii)
(b)	(ii)	(i)	(iv)	(iii)
(c)	(iv)	(i)	(iii)	(ii)
(d)	(iii)	(i)	(ii)	(iv)

123. The preservative that is added to coloured fruit squashes is:
(a) Benzoic acid   (b) Sorbic acid
(c) Sodium meta bisulphite   (d) Sodium benzonate

124. The active principle in clove is:
(a) Thymol   (b) Anethole
(c) Cineole   (d) Eugenol

125. One of the following is also known as the good cholesterol:
(a) Chylomicrons   (b) LDL
(c) VLDL   (d) HDL

Answer

120. (d) 121. (c) 122. (b) 123. (d) 124. (d)
125. (d)

126. Match the food items with their cooking properties:

List I	List II
A. Egg white	(i) Flavouring
B. Com Starch	(ii) Smoking point
C. Vanilla	(iii) Foaming
D. Oil	(iv) Thickening

Codes:	A	B	C	D
(a)	(iii)	(iv)	(i)	(ii)
(b)	(ii)	(i)	(iv)	(iii)
(c)	(iv)	(i)	(iii)	(ii)
(d)	(iii)	(i)	(ii)	(iv)

127. The correct sequence for determination of proteins by kjeldahl method is:

(i) Drying and weighing the sample
(ii) Distillation
(iii) Digestion with H_2SO_4
(iv) Titration

(a)	(i)	(iv)	(iii)	(ii)
(b)	(ii)	(i)	(iv)	(iii)
(c)	(iv)	(ii)	(i)	(iii)
(d)	(iii)	(i)	(ii)	(iv)

128. **Assertion (A):** Cloudiness occurs in clod tea.

Reason (R): It is due to the reaction of tannins and caffeine with acid.

(a) A is true but R is false
(b) Both A and R are true
(c) A is false and R is true
(d) Both A and R are false

129. **Assertion (A):** Including plenty of Fruits and Vegetables in the diet play a protective role in heart diseases.

Answer

126. (a) 127. (c) 128. (b)

Reason (R): It is attributed to the presence of fiber and antioxidants in fruits and vegetables.

(a) A is true but R is false
(b) A is false and R is true
(c) Both A and R are true
(d) Both A and R are false

130. **Assertion (A):** Night blindness in children is caused by the deficiency of vitamin A in the diet.

Reason (R): Beta-carotene is a precursor of vitamin A, so foods rich in carotene pigments should be fed to children.

(a) (A) is true but (R) is false
(b) (A) is false but (R) is true
(c) Both (A) and (R) are true
(d) Both (A) and (R) are false

131. Moisture content of dehydrated potatoes, spinach, cauliflower, ragi should be

(a) 2-8% (b) 10-16%
(c) 18-24% (d) None of these

132. Major source of energy for the body is:

(a) Protein (b) Glucose
(c) Fat (d) All of the above

133. Tocopherol is

(i) Anticaking (ii) Antioxidant
(iii) Antibiotic (iv) Vitamin

Codes:

(a) (ii) and (iv) are correct
(b) (i) and (iii) are correct
(c) (iv) and (i) are correct
(d) (iii) and (iv) are correct

134. Three forms of Vitamin D are:

Answer

129. (c) 130. (c) 131. (b) 132 (c) 133. (a)

(i) Ergocalciferol (ii) Cholecalciferol
(iii) 7-dehydrocholesterol (iv) Phytoergosterol

Find out the correct combination according to code.

(a) (ii), (iii), (iv) are correct
(b) (i), (iii), (iv) are correct
(c) (i), (ii), (iii) are correct
(d) (iv), (ii), (i) are correct

135. Meal planning is important for:

(i) Planning of food budget
(ii) Nutritional adequacy
(iii) Variety in diet
(iv) Efficient utilization of resources

Find out the correct combination according to code.

(a) (i), (ii), (iii) and (iv) are correct
(b) (i) and (ii) are correct, but (i) and iv) are incorrect
(c) (ii) and (iii) are correct, but (i) and (iv) are incorrect
(d) (i) and (iii) are correct, but (ii) and (iv) are incorrect

136. While washing fabrics of protein fibers bleeding can be prevented by:

(i) Vinegar (ii) Common salt
(iii) Washing soda (iv) Acetic acid

Codes:

(a) (i) and (iv) are correct
(b) (ii) and (iii) are correct
(c) (iii) and (iv) are correct
(d) (i) and (ii) are correct

137. **Assertion (A):** Obesity and heart disease is a result of excessive energy intake and reduced physical activity.

Reason (R): Sedentary lifestyle and availability of high energy density foods leads to degenerative disease.

Answer

134. (c) 135. (a) 136. (d)

(a) (A) is true but (R) is false
(b) (A) is false but (R) is true
(c) Both (A) and (R) are false
(d) Both (A) and (R) are true

138. Arrange the following foods in decreasing order of carotene content:

(i) Jaggery (ii) Maize
(iii) Curry leaves (iv) Pumpkin

Codes:

(a) (iv), (i), (ii), (iii) (b) (iv), (iii), (ii), (i)
(c) (iii), (ii), (i), (iv) (d) (iii), (iv), (ii), (i)

139. Identify the correct order of food supplementary programme launched by government of India:

(a) ICDS, SNP, ANP, MDMP
(b) SNP, MDMP, ANP, ICDS
(c) ANP, MDMP, SNP, ICDS
(d) ANP, SNP, ICDS, NDMP

140. Which one of the following pairs is correctly matched:

(a) Loss of liquid from solid food—Suneresis
(b) Dispersion of one liquid into another is a—Gel
(c) Colloidal system in which the solid particles are dispersed in a liquid is a—Sol
(d) Mixing of one solid particle into another is an—Emulsion

141. Match the following:

List I	List II
A. Turmeric	(i) Argemone
B. Bengal gram flour	(ii) Starch
C. Mustard	(iii) Lathyrus sativus
D. Milk	(iv) Metalin yellow
	(v) Amaranth

Answer

137. (c) 138. (c) 139. (a) 140. (b)

Codes:	A	B	C	D
(a)	(ii)	(i)	(iii)	(iv)
(b)	(ii)	(i)	(iv)	(v)
(c)	(v)	(iv)	(iii)	(i)
(d)	(iii)	(v)	(ii)	(i)

142. The emulsifying agent found in egg is:
(a) Avidin (b) Lecithin
(c) Ovaalbumin (d) Lysine

143. A cheese rich in calcium is obtained when milk is treated with:
(a) Acetic acid (b) Citric acid
(c) Rennin (d) Lipase

144. The enzymes most responsible for the digestibility of starch in the human body are:
(a) Amylases (b) Phosphatases
(c) Phosphorylase (d) Kinases

145. The most Vitamin C rich combination of vegetables and fruits is:
(a) Apple and Brinjal (b) Lemon and Cauliflower
(c) Cabbage and Oranges (d) Papaya and Potatoes

146. As directed by the Supreme Court of India the Mid-day meals served in primary schools should be:
(a) A nutritious processed food
(b) Ready to eat food
(c) A finger food
(d) Hot cooked meal

147. Match the vegetable with the pigment:

List I	List II
A. Pumpkin	(i) Anthocyanine
B. Strawberry	(ii) Carotenoids

Answer

141. (a) 142. (b) 143. (c) 144. (a) 145. (c)
146. (d)

C. Beet root		(iii) Anthoxanthins	
D. Onion		(iv) Betalins	

Codes:	A	B	C	D
(a)	(iii)	(iv)	(i)	(ii)
(b)	(ii)	(i)	(iv)	(iii)
(c)	(iv)	(i)	(iii)	(ii)
(d)	(iii)	(i)	(ii)	(iv)

148. Arrange the following foods in ascending order of their protein content:

(i) Mutton (ii) Spinach
(iii) Soyabean (iv) Whole wheat flour

Codes:

(a) (iv), (i), (ii), (iii) (b) (iv), (iii), (ii), (i)
(c) (iii), (ii), (i), (iv) (d) (ii), (iv), (i), (iii)

149. **Assertion (A):** Maillard reaction is an enzymatic reaction occurring in condensed milk.

Reason (R): This is due to the development of brown colour in a mixture of amino acid and reducing sugar.

(a) (A) is true but (R) is false
(b) (A) is false but (R) is true
(c) Both (A) and (R) are true
(d) Both (A) and (R) are false

150. **Assertion (A):** Hyperlipidaemia is generally related to an increase in the lipids of blood.

Reason (R): The use of safflower (Kardi) oil, corn-oil, or sesame oil are not preferred for hyperlipidaemic patient.

(a) (A) is true but (R) is false
(b) (A) is false but (R) is true
(c) Both (A) and (R) are true
(d) Both (A) and (R) are false

151. **Assertion (A):** Inclusion of citrus fruits in the diet is essential for the absorption of iron.

Answer

147. (c) 148. (d) 149. (c) 150. (a)

Reason (R): Vitamin C in the citrus fruit aids in the absorption of iron.

(a) (A) is true but (R) is false
(b) (A) is false but (R) is true
(c) Both (A) and (R) are true
(d) Both (A) and (R) are false

152. The Emulsifying agent found in food is:
(a) Gluten (b) Trypsin
(c) Lacithin (d) Caffeine

153. The ISO electric point of milk is:
(a) 6.6 (b) 5.6
(c) 5.2 (d) 4.6

154. Following is a sulphur containing amino acid:
(a) Lysine (b) Methionine
(c) Phenyl alanine (d) Valine

155. Strict restriction of carbohydrates is not done in a diabetic diet because it can lead to:
(a) Constipation (b) Glycos uria
(c) Ketosis (d) Steatorrhoea

156. BARS is a tool used for:
(a) Checking quality of food
(b) Designing layout plan
(c) Performance appraisal
(d) Feedback communication

157. **Assertion (A):** Scorching of milk happen on prolonged boiling.

Reason (R): The sugar and protein in milk react to give the burnt taste.

(a) (A) is true but (R) is false
(b) (A) is false but (R) is true

Answer

151. (c) 152. (c) 153. (d) 154. (b) 155. (c)
156. (c)

(c) Both (A) and (R) are true
(d) Both (A) and (R) are false

158. **Assertion (A):** Polyurethane foam is used as insulating material in refrigerators these days.

Reason (R): As it is in liquid state and set in walls of refrigerators evenly.

(a) (A) is true but (R) is false
(b) (A) is false but (R) is true
(c) Both (A) and (R) are true
(d) Both (A) and (R) are false

159. Arrange in the right sequence the stages of sugar cookery:

(i) Firm ball (ii) Soft crack
(iii) Thread (iv) Brown liquid
(v) Clear liquid

Codes:

(a) (iv), (i), (ii), (iii), (v)
(b) (iv), (iii), (ii), (i), (v)
(c) (i), (iii), (ii), (iv), (v)
(d) (iii), (iv), (ii), (i), (v)

160. Arrange the following foods in ascending order of their iron content:

(i) Egg (ii) Leafy vegetable
(iii) Liver (iv) Milk

Codes:

(a) (iv), (i), (ii), (iii) (b) (i), (iii), (iv), (ii)
(c) (iii), (ii), (i), (iv) (d) (iii), (iv), (ii), (i)

161. Match the following:

List I	List II
A. Milk	(i) Rigor Mortis
B. Apple	(ii) Maillard reaction
C. Egg	(iii) Gelatinization

Answer

157. (d) 158. (b) 159. (c) 160. (b)

D. Meat (iv) Rancidity
E. Cereal (v) Poaching
(vi) Browning reaction

Codes:	A	B	C	D	E
(a)	(iii)	(iv)	(i)	(ii)	(v)
(b)	(ii)	(i)	(iv)	(iii)	(v)
(c)	(iv)	(i)	(iii)	(ii)	(vi)
(d)	(ii)	(vi)	(v)	(i)	(iii)

162. Match the following:

List I	List II
A. Spectrophotometer	(i) Retinol
B. Soxlet Apparatus	(ii) Iron
C. HPLC	(iii) Total inorganic content
D. Muffle furnace	(iv) Oil

Codes:	A	B	C	D
(a)	(iii)	(iv)	(i)	(ii)
(b)	(ii)	(i)	(iv)	(iii)
(c)	(iv)	(i)	(iii)	(ii)
(d)	(iii)	(i)	(ii)	(iv)

163. What is the primary reason for blanching food:
(a) Cleans the food
(b) Prevents pest infestation
(c) Inactivates enzymes in food
(d) Prevents food from drying

164. Which of the following foods are rich in omega 3 fatty acids?
(i) Lard (ii) Butter
(iii) Fatty fish (iv) Olive
(v) Mustard seeds (vi) Walnut

Answer

161. (d) 162. (a) 163. (c) 164. (d)

Codes:

(a)	(v)	(ii)	(iii)
(b)	(ii)	(vi)	(iv)
(c)	(iv)	(i)	(iii)
(d)	(iii)	(v)	(vi)

165. Which of the following equipments are not used in the kitchen?

(i) Oven (ii) Cooking range
(iii) Tally machine (iv) Baine marie
(v) Blender (vi) Potato peeler

Codes:

(a) (i) and (iv) (b) (i) and (iii)
(c) (iii) and (iv) (d) (v) and (vi)

166. **Assertion (A):** Pasteurization in milk done to destroy the microbes.

Reason (R): It is tested for the presence of lactic acid in milk.

(a) (A) is true but (R) is false
(b) (A) is false but (R) is true
(c) Both (A) and (R) are true
(d) Both (A) and (R) are false

167. Give the sequence of stages of sugar cookery in making brittle.

(i) Soft ball (ii) Soft crack
(iii) Hard crack (iv) Two thread
(v) Firm ball

Codes:

(a) (i), (ii), (iii), (iv), (v)
(b) (ii), (i), (iv), (iii), (v)
(c) (iv), (i), (v), (ii), (iii)
(d) (i), (iii), (ii), (iv), (v)

Answer

165. (c) 166. (a) 167. (c)

168. Match the foods with its rich nutrients:

List I (Food)	List II (Nutrients)
A. Papaya	(i) Iron
B. Orange	(ii) Calcium
C. Dates	(iii) Vitamin C
D. Ragi	(iv) Vitamin A

Codes:	**A**	**B**	**C**	**D**
(a)	(iii)	(iv)	(i)	(ii)
(b)	(ii)	(i)	(iv)	(iii)
(c)	(iv)	(iii)	(i)	(ii)
(d)	(iii)	(i)	(ii)	(iv)

169. The S.N.F. of standard milk should be as follows:
   (a) 8.5% (b) 7.2%
   (c) 6.5% (d) 5.2%

170. The period of human embryo is:
   (a) 2-4 weeks (b) 1-8 weeks
   (c) 2-8 weeks (d) 2-6 weeks

171. Vanaspati is an adulterant in:
   (a) Malt (b) Haldi
   (c) Ghee and butter (d) Saffron

172. Which are the chemicals used for artificial ripening of fruits?
   (i) Ethephon (ii) Benzene
   (iii) Methanol (iv) Calcium carbide

   Codes:
   (a) (i) and (ii) (b) (ii) and (iii)
   (c) (iv) and (iii) (d) (iv) and (i)

173. Components of the National vitamin A prophylaxis programme are:
   (a) Providing supplementary nutrition
   (b) Distributing mega doses of Vitamin A

Answer

168. (c) 169. (a) 170. (c) 171. (c) 172. (d)

(c) feeding colostrums
(d) Encouraging consumption of fruits and veg
(e) All of the above

Codes:

(a) (i), (ii), (iii), (iv), (v) (b) (ii), (v), (iv)
(c) (i) and (iv) (d) (i), (iii), (ii), (iv), (v)

174. **Assertion (A):** Consumption of plenty of fruits and vegetables protects individuals from certain cancers.

Reason (R): The antioxidants present in fruits and vegetables help in removal of free radicals.

(a) (A) is true but (R) is false
(b) (A) is false but (R) is true
(c) Both (A) and (R) are true
(d) Both (A) and (R) are false

175. **Assertion (A):** Motion against gravity are slower than those with gravity.

Reason (R): A good example is pushing chopped vegetable into a bowl at a lower level.

(a) (A) is true but (R) is false
(b) (A) is false but (R) is true
(c) Both (A) and (R) are true
(d) Both (A) and (R) are false

176. **Assertion (A):** Bulimia nervosa is defined by little eating or reduced intake of food over a long period of time.

Reason (R): Little eating is used to describe the consumption of food that is much smaller than most people would eat during a similar period of time.

(a) (A) is true but (R) is false
(b) (A) is false but (R) is true
(c) Both (A) and (R) are true
(d) Both (A) and (R) are false

Answer

173. (c) 174. (c) 175. (c) 176. (b)

177. The protective covering on the egg shell is called:
   (a) Pericarp (b) Rennin
   (c) Cuticle (d) Epimyosin

178. The active component in clove is:
   (a) Allicin (b) Eugenol
   (c) Curricumin (d) Theaflavin

179. Additional Energy and Protein requirement during pregnancy is as follows:
   (a) 700 kals, 30 g (b) 300 kals, 15 g
   (c) 350 kals, 15 g (d) 300 kals, 30 g

180. To reduce the risk of complication, the Systolic and Diastolic Blood Pressure should be:
   (a) <120 mm Hg and <85 mm Hg
   (b) <125 mm Hg and <80 mm Hg
   (c) <80 mm Hg <120 mm Hg
   (d) <120 mm Hg <80 mm Hg

181. Which food service system produces food at a central unit and distributes processed food to other smaller units:
   (a) Commissary (b) Assembly line
   (c) Conventional (d) Cook and chill

182. Following is not an essential amino acid:
   (a) Lysine (b) Methionine
   (c) Alanine (d) Phenyl alanine

183. The iron requirement for a pregnant mother is:
   (a) 30 mg (b) 32 mg
   (c) 38 mg (d) 36 mg

184. The enzyme responsible for digestibility of fats in human body is:
   (a) Lipase (b) Amylase
   (c) Renin (d) Protease

Answer

177. (c) 178. (b) 179. (b) 180. (d) 181. (a)
182. (c) 183. (c) 184. (a)

185. Mould inhibitor used in the preparation of bread is:
   (a) Sodium chloride
   (b) Sodium and calcium propionate
   (c) Calcium carbonate
   (d) None of the above

186. Recommended allowance of Folic Acid for pregnant women is:
   (a) 300 mcg (b) 100 mcg
   (c) 500 mcg (d) 400 mcg

187. Colostrum is very good as it is rich in proteins and
   (a) Vitamins (b) Antibodies
   (c) Minerals (d) Carbohydrates

188. **Assertion (A):** The preservative added to dark coloured fruit juices is potassium meta bisulphite.

   Reason (R): This preservative is used to enhance colour.
   (a) (A) is true but (R) is false
   (b) (A) is false but (R) is true
   (c) Both (A) and (R) are true
   (d) Both (A) and (R) are false

189. **Assertion (A):** Both iron and vitamin C are required for correction/prevention of anaemia.

   Reason (R): Vitamin C helps in absorption of iron in the gut.
   (a) (A) is true but (R) is false
   (b) (A) is false but (R) is true
   (c) Both (A) and (R) are true
   (d) Both (A) and (R) are false

190. **Assertion (A):** Menu is considered as an essential tool in food service planning.

   Reason (R): Menu is a detailed list of food items served that will attract customers.

Answer

185. (b) 186. (d) 187. (b) 188. (d) 189. (c)

(a) (A) is true but (R) is false
(b) (A) is false but (R) is true
(c) Both (A) and (R) are false
(d) Both (A) and (R) are true

191. Arrange the activities in the right sequence for making cheese:

(i) Add lactic acid
(ii) Pasteurise milk
(iii) Add salt
(iv) Add bacteria on fungus
(v) Add rennin

Codes:

(a) (ii), (i), (v), (iii), (iv)
(b) (iv), (iii), (ii), (i), (v)
(c) (iii), (ii), (i), (iv), (v)
(d) (iii), (iv), (ii), (i), (v)

192. Identify statement giving the correct sequence of foods in decreasing order of calcium content:

(a) Rice, Milk, Spinach, Ragi
(b) Spinach, Ragi, Milk, Rice
(c) Milk, Ragi, Spinach, Rice
(d) Milk, Spinach, Rice, Ragi

193. Match the following:

List I	List II
A. Blanching	(i) Oil
B. Foaming	(ii) Milk
C. Emulsion	(iii) Wheat
D. Homogenization	(iv) Egg
E. Gluten formation	(v) Green Leaves
	(vi) Sugar

Codes:	A	B	C	D	E
(a)	(iii)	(iv)	(i)	(ii)	(v)
(b)	(v)	(iv)	(i)	(ii)	(iii)
(c)	(iv)	(i)	(iii)	(v)	(ii)
(d)	(iii)	(i)	(ii)	(iv)	(v)

Answer

190. (d) 191. (a) 192. (c) 193. (b)

194. **Assertion (A):** Consumption of plenty in fruits and vegetables help in the removal of free radicals.

 Reason (R): The antioxidants present in fruits and vegetables help in the removal of free radicals.

 (a) (A) is true but (R) is false
 (b) (A) is false but (R) is true
 (c) Both (A) and (R) are true
 (d) Both (A) and (R) are false

195. **Assertion (A):** Green leafy vegetables turn brown in colour on cooking.

 Reason (R): Chlorophyll pigment gets converted to phenophytin on application of heat.

 (a) (A) is true but (R) is false
 (b) (A) is false but (R) is true
 (c) Both (A) and (R) are false
 (d) Both (A) and (R) are true

196. Give the correct sequence of steps involved in bread making:

 (i) Making dough with flour
 (ii) Adding yeast to warm milk
 (iii) Punching the dough
 (iv) Rising the dough
 (v) Proofing
 (vi) Baking

 Codes:

 (a) (ii), (i), (iv), (iii), (v), (vi)
 (b) (iv), (i), (vi), (ii), (iii), (v)
 (c) (iii), (iv), (i), (ii), (vi), (v)
 (d) (i), (iii), (ii), (iv), (v), (vi)

197. Give the correct sequence of foods in decreasing order of protein content:

Answer

194. (c) 195. (d) 196. (a)

(i) Suji (ii) Moong dal
(iii) Green peas (iv) Sweet potato

Codes:

(a) (i), (ii), (iii), (iv) (b) (iv), (i), (iii), (i)
(c) (iii), (iv), (i), (ii) (d) (ii), (iii), (i), (iv)

198. Match the deficiency disease/symptom with nutrient:

List I	List II
A. Pellagra	(i) Iron
B. Beriberi	(ii) Niacin
C. Koilonechia	(iii) Ascorbic acid
D. Xerophthalmia	(iv) Retinol
	(v) Thiamine

Codes:	A	B	C	D
(a)	(iii)	(iv)	(v)	(ii)
(b)	(ii)	(i)	(iv)	(iii)
(c)	(ii)	(v)	(i)	(iv)
(d)	(iii)	(i)	(v)	(iv)

199. Cereals provide:

(i) Energy (ii) Iodine
(iii) Vitamin A (iv) Protein

Find out the correct combination according to code:

(a) (i), (ii), (iii) are correct
(b) (i) and (iv) are correct
(c) (ii) and (iv) are correct
(d) (i) and (iii) are correct

200. **Assertion (A):** In an Indian diet 70-80% of calories are derived from cereals.

Reason (R): As they are fibre rich foods.

(a) (A) is true but (R) is false
(b) (A) is false but (R) is true

Answer

197. (d) 198. (c) 199. (b) 200. (a)

(c) Both (A) and (R) are true
(d) Both (A) and (R) are false

201. The proper sequence for estimation of crude fibre in food is:
(i) Drying and weighing of food
(ii) Weighing of ground sample and defaulting
(iii) Digestion with 1.25% H_2SO_4 and filtration
(iv) Digestion with 1.25% NaOH and filtration

Codes:

(a) (ii), (iv), (i), (iii) (b) (ii), (iii), (iv), (i)
(c) (iv), (i), (iii), (ii) (d) (i), (iv), (ii), (iii)

202. Identify the correct order of ocular:
(a) Night blindness, Bitot's spot, Keratomalacia, Corneal Xerosis
(b) Bitot's spot, Keratomalacia, Corneal Xerosis, Night blindness
(c) Night blindness, Bitot's spot, Corneal Xerosis, Keratomalacia
(d) Keratomalacia, Bitot's spot, Night blindness, Corneal Xerosis

203. Which of the following foods are produced by involving lactic acid fermentation?
(i) Beer (ii) Yogurt
(iii) Cheese (iv) Vinegar

Codes:

(a) (i) and (ii) (b) (ii) and (iii)
(c) (iii) and (iv) (d) (iv) and (i)

204. Which foods do not contain gluten and is acceptable for patient with celiac disease to consume?
(i) Wheat flour (ii) Rice flour
(iii) Gram flour (iv) Corn flour

Answer

201. (c) 202. (a) 203. (b) 204. (c)

Codes:

(a) (i), (ii), (iii) (b) (ii), (i), (iv)
(c) (ii), (iii), (iv) (d) (i), (iii), (ii)

205. **Assertion (A):** Energy requirements during lactation is higher than during pregnancy.

Reason (R): As the turn over of iron is greater during lactation because of milk secretion.

(a) (A) is true but (R) is false
(b) (A) is false but (R) is true
(c) Both (A) and (R) are true
(d) Both (A) and (R) are false

206. Arrange the right sequence in decreasing order of protein content in food:

(i) Bread (ii) Cheese
(iii) Butter (iv) Boiled egg

(a) (iv), (i), (ii), (iii)
(b) (iv), (iii), (ii), (i)
(c) (iii), (ii), (i), (iv)
(d) (iv), (ii), (i), (iii)

207. Give the sequential involvement of enzymes for the digestion of food in the GIT:

(i) Iso maltase (ii) Pepsin
(iii) Ptylin (iv) Amylase

Codes:

(a) (i), (ii), (iii), (iv) (b) (ii), (i), (iv), (iii)
(c) (iii), (ii), (iv), (i) (d) (i), (iii), (ii), (iv)

208. A drop in testosterone as men age can cause:

(a) decreased energy and strength
(b) sexual dysfunction
(c) depression
(d) all of the above

Answer

205. (a) 206. (d) 207. (c) 208. (d)

Chapter 3

Clothing and Textiles

1. The gum used for printing silk with acid dyes is
   (a) Gum Arabic (b) Sodium Alignate
   (c) Synthetic thickness (d) Guar Gum
2. The dye most suitable for polyester
   (a) Azoics (b) Basic
   (c) Dispense (d) Reactive
3. If one finds loops on the underside of the seam while stitching on a sewing machine, change the:
   (a) Bobbin (b) Thread
   (c) Tension (d) Stitch length
4. One of the basic principles of design is:
   (a) Balance (b) Colour
   (c) Line (d) Size
5. **Assertion (A):** Same pattern can be used for knitted and women fabrics.

   Reason (R): Knitted and women fabrics have same properties.

   (a) (A) is true but (R) is false
   (b) (A) is false but (R) is true
   (c) Both (A) and (R) are true
   (d) Both (A) and (R) are false

Answer

1. (a) 2. (a) 3. (c) 4. (a) 5. (d)

6. Arrange the following processes in the correct order. Use the code given below:
   (i) Bundling (ii) Spreading
   (iii) Marker making (iv) Cutting

   Codes:
   (a) (i), (ii), (iii), (iv) (b) (ii), (iii), (iv), (i)
   (c) (ii), (i), (iii), (iv) (d) (ii), (iii), (i), (iv)

7. Arrange the process of weaving in the correct sequence:
   (i) Shedding (ii) Picking
   (iii) Take up (iv) Beating up

   Codes:
   (a) (i), (ii), (iii), (iv) (b) (ii), (iii), (iv), (i)
   (c) (ii), (i), (iii), (iv) (d) (ii), (iii), (i), (iv)

8. While washing fabrics of protein fibers colour bleeding can be prevented by using:
   (a) Vinegar (b) Common salt
   (c) Washing soda (d) Ammonia

9. The rays causing maximum fading of dyed fabrics are:
   (a) X-Rays (b) Infra-red rays
   (c) Ultra-violet rays (d) Red and visible light

10. Least abrasion-resistant fabric would be:
    (a) Matt (b) Gingham
    (c) Corduroy (d) Satin

11. One of the dimension of colour is:
    (a) Proportion (b) Shade
    (c) Combination of colour (d) Hue

12. **Assertion (A):** Break point of the collar is marked on the placket extension.

    Reason (R): Roll line turns back from the centre front line.

Answer

6. (b) 7. (a) 8. (a) 9. (c) 10. (d)
11. (d)

(a) (A) is true but (R) is false
(b) (A) is false but (R) is true
(c) Both (A) and (R) are true
(d) Both (A) and (R) are false

13. **Assertion (A):** In pattern making basic control dart can be shifted to any location without changing the fit of the garment.

Reason (R): Angle of the dart changes accordingly.

(a) (A) is true but (R) is false
(b) (A) is false but (R) is true
(c) Both (A) and (R) are true
(d) Both (A) and (R) are false

14. **Assertion (A):** Best method of resolving the conflict is integration.

Reason (R): Two sides reach a new solution together.

(a) (A) is true but (R) is false
(b) (A) is false but (R) is true
(c) Both (A) and (R) are true
(d) Both (A) and (R) are false

15. Give the correct sequence of attaching a facing on the neckline:

(i) Neatening the seam allowance
(ii) Stitching the facing on neckline
(iii) Slitting the seam allowance
(iv) Edge stitching the facing

Codes:

(a) (i), (iv), (iii), (ii) (b) (ii), (i), (iii), (iv)
(c) (iii), (i), (ii), (iv) (d) (ii), (iii), (i), (iv)

16. State the sequence adopted in drawing a pathway chart:

(i) Tracing the route with string
(ii) Identify the work centres

Answer

12. (c) 13. (a) 14. (c) 15. (b)

(iii) Making floor plan
(iv) Measuring the length of string

Codes:

(a) (i), (iv), (iii), (ii) (b) (i), (iii), (ii), (iv)
(c) (ii), (i), (iii), (iv) (d) (ii), (iii), (i), (iv)

17. Match the items in List I with List II:

List I	List II
A. Lycra	(i) Dubraj Das
B. Balucharies	(ii) J.P. Benberg
C. Cupra ammonium rayon	(iii) Dupont
D. Fashion adoption theory	(iv) Charles W. King

Codes:	A	B	C	D
(a)	(i)	(iv)	(iii)	(ii)
(b)	(ii)	(i)	(iv)	(iii)
(c)	(i)	(ii)	(iv)	(iii)
(d)	(iii)	(i)	(ii)	(iv)

18. Match the items in List I with List II:

List I	List II
A. Notches	(i) Front armhole
B. Single Notch	(ii) Cutting line
C. Double Notch	(iii) Stitching line
D. Balance Marks	(iv) Back armhole

Codes:	A	B	C	D
(a)	(i)	(iv)	(iii)	(ii)
(b)	(iv)	(iii)	(i)	(ii)
(c)	(i)	(ii)	(iv)	(iii)
(d)	(iii)	(i)	(ii)	(iv)

19. Following is not a direct system of yarn numbering:

(a) Cotton count (b) Denier
(c) Metric count (d) Tex

Answer

16. (d) 17. (d) 18. (b) 19. (a)

20. Series of loops that interest horizontally in a fabric are called as:
    (a) Courses (b) Wales
    (c) Warp (d) Weft
21. Preparation of the fabric for application of natural dyes is done by:
    (a) Turmeric (b) Alum
    (c) Alizarine (d) Myrobalum
22. **Assertion (A):** Rayon garments undergo progressive shrinkage.

    Reason (R): Hence care has to be taken while drying and ironing.
    (a) (A) is true but (R) is false
    (b) (A) is false but (R) is true
    (c) Both (A) and (R) are true
    (d) Both (A) and (R) are false
23. **Assertion (A):** Gores are vertical divisions within a garment

    Reason (R): They incorporate the dart shape in seams.
    (a) (A) is true but (R) is false
    (b) (A) is false but (R) is true
    (c) Both (A) and (R) are true
    (d) Both (A) and (R) are false
24. Give the correct order of applying the four support materials in the garment:
    (a) Interfacing, underlining, interlining, lining
    (b) Interlining, interfacing, underlining, lining
    (c) Underlining, interfacing, interlining, lining
    (d) Interfacing, interlining, underlining, lining
25. Match the fiber given in List I to the appearance given in List II:

Answer

20. (d) 21. (a) 22. (c) 23. (b) 24. (d)

List I	List II
A. Wool	(i) Glass rod structure
B. Linen	(ii) Scales
C. Silk	(iii) Convolutions
D. Cotton	(iv) Nodes

Codes:	A	B	C	D
(a)	(i)	(iv)	(iii)	(ii)
(b)	(i)	(ii)	(iii)	(iv)
(c)	(iv)	(i)	(iii)	(ii)
(d)	(iii)	(i)	(ii)	(iv)

26. Match the description given in List II with the terms given in List I:

List I	List II
A. Avant Garde	(i) High fashion
B. Houte Couture	(ii) Copied garment
C. Knock off	(iii) Ready to wear
D. Pret-a-Porter	(iv) Design ahead of its time

Codes:	A	B	C	D
(a)	(iv)	(i)	(ii)	(iii)
(b)	(ii)	(i)	(iv)	(iii)
(c)	(iv)	(i)	(iii)	(ii)
(d)	(iii)	(i)	(ii)	(iv)

27. The dye most suitable for polyester is:
(a) Azoics (b) Basic
(c) Disperse (d) Reactive

28. The lightest fibre is:
(a) Silk (b) Acrylic
(c) Terylene (d) Polypropylene

29. In a shoulder yoke grain line is marked:
(a) Parallel to Centre front
(b) Parallel to Centre back

Answer

25. (b) 26. (a) 27. (a) 28. (a)

(c) Perpendicular to centre front
(d) Perpendicular to centre back

30. Match the following items:

List I	List II
A. Bias binding	(i) Turning the seam easily
B. Under-stitching	(ii) Finishing the raw edge
C. Notches	(iii) Removing extra fullness from the seam
D. Stay-stitching	(iv) To retain shape

Codes:	A	B	C	D
(a)	(i)	(iv)	(iii)	(ii)
(b)	(ii)	(i)	(iii)	(iv)
(c)	(iv)	(i)	(iii)	(ii)
(d)	(iii)	(i)	(ii)	(iv)

31. Match the following:

List I	List II
A. Dubraj Das	(i) Doshalas
B. Thomas Bell	(ii) Firsh Synthetic dye
C. William Perkin	(iii) Roller printing
D. Akbar the Great	(iv) Baluchari Sarees

Codes:	A	B	C	D
(a)	(i)	(iv)	(iii)	(ii)
(b)	(ii)	(i)	(iv)	(iii)
(c)	(iv)	(i)	(iii)	(ii)
(d)	(iv)	(iii)	(ii)	(i)

32. Match the following items:

List I	List II
A. Texture	(i) Extrinsic surface enrichment of object
B. Pattern	(ii) Pictures usually of flowers and animals

Answer

29. (d) 30. (b) 31. (c)

C. Naturalistic motif	(iii) Two or three dimensional area or shapes
D. Form	(iv) Tactile quality of surface of an object

Codes:	A	B	C	D
(a)	(i)	(iv)	(iii)	(ii)
(b)	(ii)	(i)	(iv)	(iii)
(c)	(iv)	(i)	(ii)	(iii)
(d)	(iii)	(i)	(ii)	(iv)

33. Give the correct sequence in preparation of fabric for clothing construction:
    (a) Blocking, shrinking, pressing, straightening
    (b) Shrinking, straightening, blocking, pressing
    (c) Straightening, blocking, shrinking, pressing
    (d) Pressing, straightening, blocking, shrinking

34. After placing the draft on the fabric give the correct sequence followed for cutting:
    (i) Marking seam allowances
    (ii) Marking the stitching line
    (iii) Cutting on seam allowances
    (iv) Tracing the stitching line

Codes:

(a)	(i)	(iv)	(iii)	(ii)
(b)	(ii)	(i)	(iv)	(iii)
(c)	(iv)	(ii)	(i)	(iii)
(d)	(iii)	(i)	(ii)	(iv)

35. **Assertion (A):** A dart in a bodice block can be shifted from one location to another without changing the fit of the garment.

    Reason (R): Fit remains unchanged as the angle of the dart remains the same.

Answer

32. (c) 33. (b) 34. (c)

(a) (A) is true but (R) is false
(b) (A) is false but (R) is true
(c) Both (A) and (R) are true
(d) Both (A) and (R) are false

36. **Assertion (A):** There is more shrinkage towards the length of the fabric.

Reason (R): Warp yarns are stretched while on the loom.

(a) (A) is true but (R) is false
(b) (A) is false but (R) is true
(c) Both (A) and (R) are true
(d) Both (A) and (R) are false

37. **Assertion (A):** Solar energy is termed as non-renewable energy.

Reason (R): It is an energy that can be conserved by using black coloured apparatus.

(a) (A) is true but (R) is false
(b) (A) is false but (R) is true
(c) Both (A) and (R) are true
(d) Both (A) and (R) are false

38. A layout that is inappropriate for unidirectional fabric is:

(a) Lengthwise fold (b) Crosswise fold
(c) Open fold (d) Double fold

39. In a pattern darts can be replaced by:

(i) Gathers (ii) Pin tucks
(iii) Style line (iv) Control seam

Codes:

(a) (ii) and (i) are correct
(b) (ii) and (iii) are correct
(c) (iii) and (iv) are correct
(d) (i) and (iv) are correct

Answer

35. (d) 36. (b) 37. (a) 38. (b) 39. (c)

40. **Assertion (A):** In a seam slits are given in onward curve.

Reason (R): Smaller area falls over bigger area.

(a) (A) is true but (R) is false
(b) (A) is false but (R) is true
(c) Both (A) and (R) are true
(d) Both (A) and (R) are false

41. **Assertion (A):** Basket, ribbed, twill and satin are all basic weaves.

Reason (R): In all these weaves third set of yarn is used.

(a) (A) is true but (R) is false
(b) (A) is false but (R) is true
(c) Both (A) and (R) are false
(d) Both (A) and (R) are true

42. Give the correct sequence of steps follow while dyeing:

(i) After treatment
(ii) Preparation of fabric
(iii) Preparation of dye bath
(iv) Addition of exhaustion agents

Codes:

(a) (iv), (i), (ii), (iii) (b) (ii), (iii), (iv), (i)
(c) (iii), (ii), (i), (iv) (d) (iii), (iv), (ii), (i)

43. Give the correct threading sequence pattern of a sewing machine:

(i) Needle (ii) Spool
(iii) Thread take up lever (iv) Tension discs

Codes:

(a) (iv), (i), (ii), (iii) (b) (iv), (iii), (ii), (i)
(c) (iii), (ii), (i), (iv) (d) (ii), (iv), (iii), (i)

44. Arrange the following household activities on the basis of energy cost from light to very heavy:

Answer

40. (a) 41. (d) 42. (b) 43. (d)

(i) Mopping floor (ii) Dusting furniture
(iii) Grinding masala manually (iv) Ironing clothes

Codes:

(a) (ii), (iv), (i), (iii) (b) (iv), (iii), (ii), (i)
(c) (iii), (ii), (i), (iv) (d) (iii), (iv), (ii), (i)

45. Match the machine parts given in List I with their functions given in List II:

List I	List II
A. Pressure feet	(i) Pushes fabric ahead after stitching
B. Feet dog	(ii) Provides smooth surface while stitching
C. Throat plate	(iii) Holds the fabric in place during stitching
D. Face plate	(iv) Indicates the threading chart

Codes:	A	B	C	D
(a)	(iii)	(iv)	(i)	(ii)
(b)	(ii)	(i)	(iv)	(iii)
(c)	(iv)	(ii)	(i)	(iii)
(d)	(iii)	(i)	(ii)	(iv)

46. Match the fabrics given below in List I and List II with their characteristics given:

List I	List II
A. Knits	(i) Open work
B. Wovens	(ii) Web structure
C. Felt	(iii) Warps and wefts
D. Lace	(iv) Wales and courses

Codes:	A	B	C	D
(a)	(iii)	(ii)	(i)	(iv)
(b)	(ii)	(i)	(iv)	(iii)
(c)	(iv)	(i)	(iii)	(ii)
(d)	(iii)	(i)	(ii)	(iv)

Answer

44. (a) 45. (c) 46. (a)

47. Double pointed dart is called:
    (a) French (b) Flange
    (c) Fish (d) Dressmakers

48. Match the items in List I with List II:

List I	List II
A. Designer darts	(i) Partially stitched darts
B. French darts	(ii) Darts coming till the apex
C. Flange darts	(iii) Darts at the lower shoulder point
D. Dart tuck	(iv) Darts on the side seam closer to the waist line

Codes:	A	B	C	D
(a)	(iii)	(iv)	(i)	(ii)
(b)	(ii)	(i)	(iv)	(iii)
(c)	(iv)	(i)	(iii)	(ii)
(d)	(iii)	(i)	(ii)	(iv)

49. Match the following:

List I	List II
A. Drafting requires	(i) Coconut
B. Softness or roughness	(ii) Nylon
C. Fabric suitable for travel	(iii) Texture
D. Coir is obtained from	(iv) Details

Codes:	A	B	C	D
(a)	(iii)	(iv)	(i)	(ii)
(b)	(iv)	(iii)	(ii)	(i)
(c)	(iv)	(i)	(iii)	(ii)
(d)	(iii)	(i)	(ii)	(iv)

50. Match the colour scheme in List I and List II with the given colours:

List I	List II
A. Triad	(i) Green and red
B. Complementary	(ii) Blue, slate blue

Answer

47. (c) 48. (d) 49. (b)

C. Monochromatic (iii) Yellow and green
D. Analogous (iv) Yellow, blue, red

Codes:	A	B	C	D
(a)	(iii)	(iv)	(i)	(ii)
(b)	(ii)	(i)	(iv)	(iii)
(c)	(iv)	(i)	(ii)	(iii)
(d)	(iii)	(i)	(ii)	(iv)

51. Give the right order of steps followed while dyeing:
    (i) After treatments
    (ii) Preparation of fabric
    (iii) Preparation of dye bath
    (iv) Addition of exhaustive agents

    Codes:
    (a) (ii), (iii), (iv), (i) (b) (iv), (iii), (ii), (i)
    (c) (iii), (ii), (i), (iv) (d) (iii), (iv), (ii), (i)

52. Give the correct sequence of preparing the petal sleeve for attachment:
    (i) Finish lower round arm
    (ii) Stitch under arm seam
    (iii) Match the sleeve notches with the armhole notches
    (iv) Overlap the sleeve at the centre line

    Codes:
    (a) (iv), (i), (ii), (iii) (b) (i), (ii), (iii), (iv)
    (c) (iii), (ii), (i), (iv) (d) (iii), (iv), (ii), (i)

53. Give the right order of home management process:
    (i) Energising (ii) Evaluation
    (iii) Planning (iv) Adjusting
    (v) Checking

    Codes:
    (a) (iii), (i), (v), (iv), (ii) (b) (iv), (iii), (ii), (i), (v)
    (c) (iii), (ii), (i), (iv), (v) (d) (iii), (iv), (ii), (i), (v)

Answer

50. (c) 51. (a) 52. (b) 53. (a)

54. **Assertion (A):** Slim skirt is considered a primary block.

    Reason (R): It can be adapted to any style of skirts.

    (a) (A) is true but (R) is false
    (b) (A) is false but (R) is true
    (c) Both (A) and (R) are true
    (d) Both (A) and (R) are false

55. **Assertion (A):** The grain in a woven fabric can be identified by the degree of stretch along the years.

    Reason (R): Warp yarns stretch more in comparison to weft yarns.

    (a) (A) is true but (R) is false
    (b) (A) is false but (R) is true
    (c) Both (A) and (R) are true
    (d) Both (A) and (R) are false

56. A dress is most visually pleasing if it is divided into:

    (a) Two equal parts (b) Three equal parts
    (c) Unequal parts (d) Four equal parts

57. Drapability of the costume is more pleasing with:

    (a) Straight grain (b) Off grain
    (c) True bias grain (d) None of these

58. Spandex fibre is:

    (a) Crease resistant fibre (b) Water proof fibre
    (c) Elastomeric fibre (d) Flame retardant fibre

59. Shrinkage of cotton fabrics is reduced by the process:

    (a) Felting (b) Mercerisation
    (c) Sanforization (d) Calendering

60. Analogous colour scheme makes use of following colours in a colour wheel:

    (a) Two or three colours adjacent to each other
    (b) Two colours opposite to each other

Answer

54. (b) 55. (a) 56. (a) 57. (c) 58. (c)
59. (a)

(c) Three colours forming a triangle
(d) Half of colour wheel

61. **Assertion (A):** In pattern making waist line dart can be shifted to any location without changing the fit of the garment.

Reason (R): Angle of the dart changes accordingly.

(a) (A) is true but (R) is false
(b) (A) is false but (R) is true
(c) Both (A) and (R) are true
(d) Both (A) and (R) are false

62. **Assertion (A):** Direct dyes bleed while washing.

Reason (R): Therefore direct dyed fabrics are after treated with cationic agents.

(a) (A) is true but (R) is false
(b) (A) is false but (R) is true
(c) Both (A) and (R) are true
(d) Both (A) and (R) are false

63. Write down the correct sequence in preparation of fabric for clothing construction:

(i) Blocking (ii) Shrinking
(iii) Pressing (iv) Straightening

Codes:

(a) (iv), (i), (ii), (iii) (b) (ii), (iv), (i), (iii)
(c) (iii), (ii), (i), (iv) (d) (iii), (iv), (ii), (i)

64. Correct the sequence for the preparation of screen for printing:

(i) Tracing the design and application of screen for printing
(ii) Exposure to Sunlight/Artificial light
(iii) Coating with emulsion and drying
(iv) Washing the screen

Answer

60. (b) 61. (d) 62. (c) 63. (b)

Codes:

(a) (iv), (i), (ii), (iii) (b) (iv), (iii), (ii), (i)
(c) (iii), (iv), (i), (ii) (d) (iii), (iv), (ii), (i)

65. Match the following List I with List II:

List I	List II
A. Polyamide fibre	(i) Filament
B. Yarn number	(ii) Nylon
C. Pile weave	(iii) Coconut
D. Strand of long fibres	(iv) Velvet

Codes:	A	B	C	D
(a)	(iii)	(iv)	(i)	(ii)
(b)	(ii)	(iii)	(iv)	(i)
(c)	(iv)	(i)	(iii)	(ii)
(d)	(iii)	(i)	(ii)	(iv)

66. Which of the following holds the bobbin in the sewing machine?
(a) Feed dog (b) Pressure foot
(c) Oscillating hook (d) Thread take up lever

67. Which of the following does not represent Kasuti Embroidery?
(a) Menthi (b) Aari
(c) Gavanti (d) Murgi

68. Correct layouts of unidirectional fabrics for garment cutting are:
(i) Crosswise fold (ii) Lengthwise fold
(iii) Double fold (iv) Open fold

Codes:

(a) (i), (ii) and (iii) are correct
(b) (ii), (iii) and (iv) are correct
(c) (i), (iii) and (iv) are correct
(d) (i), (ii) and (iv) are correct

Answer

64. (c) 65. (b) 66. (c) 67. (b) 68. (b)

69. Following are novelty yarns:

(i) Crepe yarn (ii) Boucle yarn
(iii) Slub yarn (iv) Flock yarn

Codes:

(a) (i), (ii) and (iv) are correct
(b) (i), (iii) and (iv) are correct
(c) (i), (ii) and (iii) are correct
(d) (ii), (iii) and (iv) are correct

70. **Assertion (A):** Both garment bias and true bias can be used for finishing necklines.

Reason (R): Both have same amount of stretch.

(a) (A) is true but (R) is false
(b) (A) is false but (R) is true
(c) Both (A) and (R) are true
(d) Both (A) and (R) are false

71. **Assertion (A):** Cross dyeing and union dyeing are same.

Reason (R): Both may produce multicoloured effects.

(a) (A) is true but (R) is false
(b) (A) is false but (R) is true
(c) Both (A) and (R) are true
(d) Both (A) and (R) are false

72. Give the correct sequence for applying the following in a garment:

(i) Interlining (ii) Interfacing
(iii) Underlining (iv) Lining

Codes:

(a) (i), (ii), (iii), (iv) (b) (ii), (i), (iv), (iii)
(c) (iii), (iv), (i), (ii) (d) (ii), (iii), (i), (iv)

73. Give the right order of removing lipstick stain from fabric:

Answer

69. (d) 70. (d) 71. (b) 72. (d)

(i) Wash in hot soapy water
(ii) Sponge with a grease solvent
(iii) Bleach the stain
(iv) Rinse in hot water and dry in sun

Codes:

(a) (i), (ii), (iii), (iv) (b) (ii), (i), (iii), (iv)
(c) (iii), (iv), (i), (ii) (d) (i), (iii), (ii), (iv)

74. How many colours classified? Indicate the right sequence:
(a) Secondary, primary, intermediate, tertiary, quaternary
(b) Binary, primary, intermediate, quaternary, tertiary
(c) Primary, secondary, intermediate, tertiary, quaternary
(d) Binary, secondary, intermediate, tertiary, quaternary

75. Match the following:

List I	List II
A. Diagonal basting	(i) Permanent stitch
B. Hemming	(ii) Functional as well as decorative
C. Herring bone stitch	(iii) Temporary stitch
D. Buttonhole stitch	(iv) Decorative stitch

Codes:	A	B	C	D
(a)	(iii)	(i)	(iv)	(ii)
(b)	(ii)	(i)	(iv)	(iii)
(c)	(iv)	(i)	(iii)	(ii)
(d)	(iii)	(i)	(ii)	(iv)

76. Match the List I with List II:

List I	List II
A. Wale	(i) Series of loops extending crosswise
B. Weft	(ii) Longitudinal yarns
C. Warp	(iii) Crosswise yarns
D. Courses	(iv) Column of loops parallel to length

Answer

73. (b) 74. (c) 75. (a)

Codes:	A	B	C	D
(a)	(iii)	(iv)	(i)	(ii)
(b)	(ii)	(i)	(iv)	(iii)
(c)	(iv)	(iii)	(ii)	(i)
(d)	(iii)	(i)	(ii)	(iv)

77. Degree of polymerization for polyester ranges between
    (a) 50-70 (b) 90-115
    (c) 115-140 (d) 140-165
78. Which of the following can finish hundreds of garments at one time by a single operator?
    (a) Carousel jeans finisher
    (b) Steam dolly
    (c) Tunnel finisher
    (d) Suction counter table
79. To avoid diaper rash:
    (i) Change wet diapers immediately
    (ii) Use soft pants on diapers
    (iii) Avoid using diapers till rashes disappear
    (iv) Clean and dry the area before putting a fresh diaper

    Codes:
    (a) (i) and (ii) are correct
    (b) (i), (iii) and (iv) are correct
    (c) (ii) and (iii) are correct
    (d) (i) and (iv) are correct
80. Following tests are mandatory for exports of children's clothing:
    (i) Zipper strength (ii) Snap strength
    (iii) Needle detection (iv) Seam strength

    Codes:
    (a) (i), (ii) and (iii) are correct
    (b) (ii), (iii) and (iv) are correct

Answer

76. (c) 77. (c) 78. (c) 79. (d)

(c) (i), (iii) and (iv) are correct
(d) (i), (ii) and (iv) are correct

81. Which of the following blends have best flame retardancy?

(i) Cotton - Wool
(ii) Cotton - Spandex
(iii) Modacrylic - Spandex
(iv) Modacrylic - Wool
(v) Aramid - PVC

Codes:

(a) (i) and (ii) are correct
(b) (iv) and (v) are correct
(c) (i) and (iii) are correct
(d) (ii) and (iv) are correct

82. Which of the following thread packages are not suitable for use on industrial machines?

(i) Spools
(ii) Cops
(iii) Vicones
(iv) Cones

Codes:

(a) (i) and (iii)
(b) (ii) and (iii)
(c) (i) and (ii)
(d) (iii) and (iv)

83. Which among the following are advertised under 'classified category'?

(i) Job vacancy
(ii) Matrimonial
(iii) Coffee powder
(iv) Bicycles

Codes:

(a) (i) and (ii) are correct
(b) (ii) and (iv) are correct
(c) (iii) and (iv) are correct
(d) (i) and (iii) are correct

84. **Assertion (A):** A dart can be relocated without changing the fit.

Reason (R): Shifting of dart to various places does not change the angle of dart.

(a) (A) is true but (R) is false
(b) (A) is false but (R) is true

Answer

80. (b) 81. (b) 82. (c) 83. (a)

(c) Both (A) and (R) are true
(d) Both (A) and (R) are false

85. **Assertion (A):** To identify the polyester fibre it is important to negate the presence of nylon and acrylic by dissolving in hot phenol and concentrated nitric acid.

Reason (R): Polyester is insoluble in both hot phenol and concentrated nitric acid.

(a) (A) is true but (R) is false
(b) (A) is false but (R) is true
(c) Both (A) and (R) are true
(d) Both (A) and (R) are false

86. Bright coloured clothes express:
(a) Confidence (b) Disturbed mind
(c) Happiness (d) Lack of confidence

87. Shears are used for cutting:
(a) Cloth (b) Leaf
(c) Paper (d) Metal

88. Jute is called as:
(a) Aluminium fibre (b) Silver fibre
(c) Copper fibre (d) Golden fibre

89. The part of pineapple plant used for fabric manufacturing process is:
(a) Flowers (b) Leaf
(c) Stem (d) Root

90. Which of the following governs the selection of needle:
(a) Type of thread (b) Type of fabric
(c) Stitch length (d) Tension of thread

91. Which of the following is not a design repeat:
(a) Drop (b) Rotary
(c) Satin (d) Mirror

Answer

84. (c) 85. (c) 86. (c) 87. (a) 88. (d)
89. (b) 90. (b) 91. (b)

92. Which of the following dart is drawn till the pivot point:
   (a) French dart (b) Fish dart
   (c) Designers dart (d) Dressmakers dart

93. The pocket that is applied on the surface of the garment is:
   (a) Kangaroo pocket (b) Welt pocket
   (c) Yoke pocket (d) Bound pocket

94. Which dart is a double pointed dart:
   (a) French dart (b) Flange dart
   (c) Fish dart (d) Designers dart

95. Diagonal ridges are characteristic feature of which weave?
   (a) Twill (b) Dobby
   (c) Swivel (d) Jacquard

96. Which of the following is sheared from a living sheep?
   (a) Flannel (b) Felt
   (c) Fleece (d) Moire

97. **Assertion (A):** Puckering takes place while machine stitching.

   Reason (R): Use of improper needle and thread tension.
   (a) (A) is true but (R) is false
   (b) (A) is false but (R) is true
   (c) Both (A) and (R) are true but (R) is not correct explanation
   (d) Both (A) and (R) are false

98. **Assertion (A):** Value addition includes Dyeing.

   Reason (R): Dyeing is a form of applying colour using blocks.
   (a) (A) is true but (R) is false
   (b) (A) is false but (R) is true
   (c) Both (A) and (R) are true
   (d) Both (A) and (R) are false

Answer

92. (b) 93. (a) 94. (c) 95. (a) 96. (c)
97. (c) 98. (a)

99. Garment construction includes the sequence of:
   (i) Body measurement
   (ii) Surface enrichment
   (iii) Drafting and pattern making
   (iv) Joining of front and back
   (v) Insertion of darts and fullness

   Codes:

   (a) (ii), (i), (v), (iii), (iv)   (b) (i), (iii), (iv), (v), (ii)
   (c) (iii), (ii), (i), (iv), (v)   (d) (iii), (iv), (ii), (i), (v)

100. Arrange the right sequence of weaving process:
   (i) Shedding   (ii) Picking
   (iii) Take up   (iv) Beating

   Codes:

   (a) (iv), (i), (ii), (iii)   (b) (iv), (iii), (ii), (i)
   (c) (iii), (ii), (i), (iv)   (d) (i), (ii), (iii), (iv)

101. Match the following items:

List I	List II
A. Bias binding	(i) Turning the seam easily
B. Under stitching	(ii) Finishing the raw edges
C. Notches	(iii) Removing extra fullness from the seam
D. Stay stitching	(iv) To retain the shape

Codes:	A	B	C	D
(a)	(iii)	(iv)	(i)	(ii)
(b)	(ii)	(i)	(iv)	(iii)
(c)	(ii)	(i)	(iii)	(iv)
(d)	(iii)	(i)	(ii)	(iv)

102. Match the following:

List I	List II
A. Acrylic	(i) Modified Basic dyes
B. Silk	(ii) Disperse dyes

Answer

99. (b)   100. (d)   101. (c)

C. Polyester (iii) Acid dyes
D. Cotton (iv) Pigment dyes

Codes:	A	B	C	D
(a)	(i)	(iv)	(ii)	(iii)
(b)	(ii)	(i)	(iv)	(iii)
(c)	(iv)	(i)	(iii)	(ii)
(d)	(iii)	(i)	(ii)	(iv)

103. **Assertion (A):** Surface designing includes printing.

Reason (R): Printing is a form of applying colour all over the fabric.

(a) (A) is true but (R) is false
(b) (A) is false but (R) is true
(c) Both (A) and (R) are true
(d) Both (A) and (R) are false

104. **Assertion (A):** In a seam notches are given in an outward curve.

Reason (R): Smaller area falls over bigger area.

(a) (A) is true but (R) is false
(b) (A) is false but (R) is true
(c) Both (A) and (R) are true
(d) Both (A) and (R) are false

105. Give the sequence of preparation of fabric for cutting:

(a) Blocking, straightening, marking, pressing
(b) Pressing, blocking, straightening, marking
(c) Straightening, blocking, pressing, marking
(d) Marking, pressing, straightening, blocking

106. Give the correct sequence of processing the line fibre:

(a) Rippling, Retting, Scutching, Hackling
(b) Scutching, Rippling, Retting, Hackling
(c) Hackling, Rippling, Retting, Scutching
(d) Retting, Rippling, Scutching, Hackling

Answer

102. (a) 103. (a) 104. (b) 105. (b) 106. (d)

107. Match the following given in List I with List II:

List I	List II
A. Fabrics with wavy pattern	(i) Cire
B. Wrinkled fabric	(ii) Plisse
C. Highly polished fabric	(iii) Suede
D. Fuzzed surface fabric	(iv) Moire

Codes:	A	B	C	D
A	(iii)	(iv)	(ii)	(i)
B	(ii)	(i)	(iv)	(iii)
C	(iv)	(i)	(iii)	(ii)
D	(iii)	(i)	(ii)	(iv)

108. Match the effect given in List II to the finish mentioned in List I:

List I	List II
A. Parchmentization	(i) After lustre
B. Beetling	(ii) Alter drape
C. Embossing	(iii) Raises fibre surface
D. Gigging	(iv) Creates textures

Codes:	A	B	C	D
(a)	(iii)	(iv)	(i)	(ii)
(b)	(ii)	(i)	(iii)	(iv)
(c)	(ii)	(i)	(iv)	(iii)
(d)	(iii)	(i)	(ii)	(iv)

109. Chemical finishes exclusively given to cotton to increase lustre, strength and dyeability are:

(i) Fulling (ii) Crabbing
(iii) Bleaching (iv) Mercerization

Find the correct combination according to code:

(a) (i) and (iii) are correct
(b) (iii) and (iv) are correct

Answer

107. (a) 108. (c)

(c) (i) and (iv) are correct
(d) (ii) and (iii) are correct

110. **Assertion (A):** Use of mordants is essential while using any type of dye.

Reason (R): Mordant increases the colour fastness of the dye.

(a) (A) is true but (R) is false
(b) (A) is false but (R) is true
(c) Both (A) and (R) are false
(d) Both (A) and (R) are true

111. **Assertion (A):** Decorative yoke can be cut on any grain of the fabric.

Reason (R): It supports the weight of the garment.

(a) (A) is true but (R) is false
(b) (A) is false but (R) is true
(c) Both (A) and (R) are true
(d) Both (A) and (R) are false

112. In a pattern, darts can be replaced by:

(i) Tucks (ii) Gather
(iii) Style line (iv) Control seam

Codes:

(a) (i) and (iii) are correct
(b) (ii) and (iii) are correct
(c) (ii) and (iv) are correct
(d) (ii, (iii) and (iv) are correct

113. Which of the following methods of printing are currently practised largely in the Indian textile industry?

(i) Screen Printing (ii) Digital
(iii) Roller Printing (iv) Block Printing

Codes:

(a) (i) and (iii) are correct
(b) (i), (ii) and (iv) are correct

Answer

109. (b) 110. (d) 111. (c) 112. (c)

(c) (i), (ii) and (iii) are correct
(d) (ii), (iii) and (iv) are correct

114. Which among the following are neutral colours?

(i) Black (ii) Red
(iii) Green (iv) White

Codes:

(a) (i), (ii) and (iii) are correct
(b) (iii) and (iv) are correct
(c) (i) and (iv) are correct
(d) (ii), (iii) and (iv) are correct

115. **Assertion (A):** Break-point of the collar is marked on the placket extension.

Reason (R): Roll line turns back from the centre front line.

(a) (R) is true but (A) is false
(b) (R) is false but (A) is true
(c) Both (A) and (R) are true
(d) Both (A) and (R) are false

116. **Assertion (A):** Brocade, Huckaback, Jacquard and Tapestry can be classified under same category.

Reason (R): All can be made on the Jacquard loom.

(a) (A) is true but (R) is false
(b) (A) is false but (R) is true
(c) Both (A) and (R) are true
(d) Both (A) and (R) are false

117. Give the right sequence of producing synthetic fibres:

(i) Treatment with finishing chemicals
(ii) Extrusion
(iii) Polymerization
(iv) Dissolving in solution

Answer

113. (b) 114. (c) 115. (b) 116. (d)

Codes:

(a) (iii), (iv), (ii), (i) (b) (ii), (i), (iv), (iii)
(c) (iii), (iv), (i), (ii) (d) (i), (iii), (ii), (iv)

118. Match the fashion terms given with their meanings:

List I	List II
A. Classic	(i) Exclusive custom fitted clothing
B. Fad	(ii) Ready to wear
C. Haute-couture	(iii) Last through ages
D. Pret-a-porter	(iv) Short lived craze

Codes:	A	B	C	D
(a)	(iv)	(iii)	(i)	(ii)
(b)	(iii)	(iv)	(i)	(ii)
(c)	(iv)	(i)	(iii)	(ii)
(d)	(iii)	(i)	(ii)	(iv)

119. Match the following:

List I	List II
A. Cotton	(i) Plant stem
B. Pineapple	(ii) Seed hair
C. Flax	(iii) Plant leaf
D. Coir	(iv) Fruit husk

Codes:	A	B	C	D
(a)	(ii)	(iii)	(i)	(iv)
(b)	(ii)	(i)	(iii)	(iv)
(c)	(iv)	(ii)	(iii)	(i)
(d)	(i)	(iii)	(ii)	(iv)

Answer

117. (a) 118. (b) 119. (a)

Chapter 4

Research Methodology

1. "Method means the logical process used in discovering or in demonstrating the truth" said by:
   (a) Aristotle (b) G.K. Zipf
   (c) C. Shannon (d) Cossa
2. "Science goes with the method, not with the subject matter" said by:
   (a) Newton (b) Stuart Chase
   (c) H.E. Bliss (d) Bradford
3. What does KM stand for:
   (a) Keyboard
   (b) Kilo Metre
   (c) Knowledge Management
   (d) Karl Marx
4. Panel Survey methods is a direct extension of:
   (a) Interview sampling
   (b) Case study
   (c) Sampling technique
   (d) Data collection
5. In Research Design which is considered as the most important component?
   (a) Case study
   (b) Review of literature

Answer

1. (d) 2. (b) 3. (c) 4. (a)

(c) Observation
(d) Formation of hypothesis

6. In Historical Method of research, the data collection is done through using questionnaire technique.
   (a) True (b) False
7. The third step of Research Methodology is:
   (a) Selection and Analysis of Problem
   (b) Data Collection
   (c) Analysis of Data
   (d) Report Writing
8. Which of the following is the research tool:
   (a) Interview
   (b) Questionnaire
   (c) Both (a) and (b)
   (d) None of these
9. The characteristic of research is:
   (a) Continuous process
   (b) Systematic
   (c) Follow Rigorous standards
   (d) All the above
10. Mark the odd one:
    (a) Experimental research design
    (b) Diagnostic research design
    (c) Exploratory research design
    (d) Applied research design
11. 'Einstein's theory of relativity' is an example of:
    (a) Historical research
    (b) Seminal research
    (c) Fundamental research
    (d) Experimental research

Answer

5. (d) 6. (b) 7. (c) 8. (c) 9. (d)
10. (d) 11. (b)

12. 'Spiral of Scientific Method' is an example of:
    (a) Pure research
    (b) Historical research
    (c) Inductive research
    (d) Deductive research
13. Who defines that "knowledge is the consequence of a filterized process through intellectual system"?
    (a) J.H. Shera (b) Ackaff
    (c) Lamare (d) S.R. Ranganathan
14. "Knowledge is the sum total of information conserved by civilization" said by:
    (a) Ackaff (b) A.J. Lotka
    (c) Karl Marx (d) S.R. Ranganathan
15. Match the following:

(1) Data	(i) Cotton
(2) Information	(ii) Yarn
(3) Knowledge	(iii) Cloth

    Codes:
    (a) 1(i), 2(ii), 3(iii) (b) 1(ii), 2(i), 3(iii)
    (c) 1(i), 2(iii), 3(ii) (d) 1(iii), 2(ii), 3(i)
16. Scientific method of research can be used:
    (a) Only in humanities
    (b) Only in science
    (c) Only in social science
    (d) In all the disciplines
17. Historical method of research can be applied:
    (a) Only in history
    (b) Only in humanities
    (c) Only in science
    (d) In all the disciplines

Answer

12. (c) 13. (a) 14. (d) 15. (a) 16. (d)
17. (d)

18. Experimental research is:
    (a) Present oriented research
    (b) Future oriented research
    (c) Free-fundamental research
    (d) Priori oriented research

19. Survey research is:
    (a) Present oriented research
    (b) Future oriented research
    (c) Priori oriented research
    (d) Free-fundamental research

20. Research starts from Nadir and ends at:
    (a) Nadir (b) Zenith
    (c) Ascendant (d) Descendant

21. The famous book *Logic* was written by Hegel and published in the year:
    (a) 1800 (b) 1812
    (c) 1847 (d) 1849

22. The main step of Scientific Method is:
    1. Selection and analysis of problem
    2. Formulation of Hypothesis
    3. Data Collection
    4. Preparation of report

    Codes:
    (a) 1, 3, 4 (b) 2, 3, 4
    (c) 1, 2, 3 (d) All the above

23. Who define that "Design is the process of making decision before the situation arises in which the decision is to be carried out"?
    (a) Hegel (b) A.L. Edward
    (c) Ackaff (d) S.R. Ranganathan

Answer

18. (b) 19. (a) 20. (a) 21. (b) 22. (d)
23. (c)

24. Formal and Informal Text are carried out in:
    (a) Diagnostic research design
    (b) Experimental research design
    (c) Exploratory research design
    (d) Applied research design
25. Academic object and Utilitarian object are two folds of:
    (a) Social science research
    (b) Applied research
    (c) Seminal research
    (d) Content analysis research
26. Normative principles is given by Ranganathan, it is based on:
    (a) Historical research (b) Scientific research
    (c) Survey research (d) Statistical research
27. What is hypothesis?
    (a) A tentative
    (b) Plan of study
    (c) An important instrument of research
    (d) All the above
28. Null Hypothesis is started:
    (a) Negatively (b) Positively
    (c) Both (a) and (b) (d) Neither (a) nor (b)
29. Who define that "Hypothesis is suggested answer to a problem"?
    (a) J.B. Best (b) W. Cleverdon
    (c) Town Sand (d) A.L. Edward
30. "A hypothesis is a nature of the relationship between two or more variable, it is an alternative answer to the question" said by:
    (a) Town Sand (b) A.L. Edward
    (c) S.R. Ranganathan (d) J.B. Best

Answer

24. (a) 25. (a) 26. (b) 27. (d) 28. (a)
29. (c) 30. (b)

31. The famous book *The Republic* was written by:
   (a) Ackaff (b) Aristotle
   (c) Plato (d) Karl Marx

32. Who discovcred the concept of Zero?
   (a) Karl Marx (b) Plato
   (c) Aryabhatta (d) Vivekanand

33. The concept of Fundamental Categories is enunciated by:
   (a) J.H. Shera (b) F. Rider
   (c) Melvil Dewey (d) S.R. Ranganathan

34. Science is a systematized positive knowledge or that branch of study which is concerned with a connected body of demonstrated truth.
   (a) True (b) False

35. Who defines that "Science is partially unified knowledge"?
   (a) Plato (b) Marx
   (c) Edward (d) Ranganathan

36. Match the following:

(1) Experimental Research	(i) Cranfield studies
(2) Applied Research	(ii) Five laws of library science
(3) Inductive Research	(iii) Chain procedure
(4) Fundamental Research	(iv) Spiral of scientific method

   Codes:
   (a) 1(i), 2(iii), 3(iv), 4(ii) (b) 1(i), 2(ii), 3(iii), 4(iv)
   (c) 1(i), 2(ii), 3(iv), 4(iii) (d) 1(i), 2(iii), 3(ii), 4(iv)

37. 'Controlled Group' is a term, which is used in:
   (a) Interview method
   (b) Scientific research
   (c) Survey research
   (d) Experimental research

Answer

31. (c) 32. (c) 33. (d) 34. (a) 35. (a)
36. (a) 37. (d)

38. Delphi Technique is related with:
    (a) Data analysis
    (b) Data collection
    (c) Data dissemination
    (d) Data processing

39. 'Ramanujam theory of Mathematics' is an example of:
    (a) Bibliomatrics method
    (b) Historical method
    (c) Seminal research
    (d) Scientific research

40. Who is the author of *Leviathan*?
    (a) Thomas Hobbes (b) H. Spencer
    (c) P. Louis (d) R.F. Clark

41. Who is the father of Liberalism?
    (a) Bradford (b) John Locke
    (c) Thomas Hobbes (d) Ranganathan

42. Who is the father of Absolution?
    (a) Thomas Hobbes (b) A.L. Edward
    (c) B. Lemarc (d) S.R. Ranganathan

43. Which of the following technique is not employed in Bibliomatrics?
    (a) Ranking (b) Citing
    (c) Counting (d) Measuring

44. British Association for Advertisement of Science is located at:
    (a) Paris (b) Chicago
    (c) Cambridge (d) London

45. The book *Classification of Sciences* was written by:
    (a) Charles Darwin (b) Bacon
    (c) Herbert Spencer (d) Ranganathan

Answer

38. (b) 39. (c) 40. (a) 41. (b) 42. (a)
43. (d) 44. (c) 45. (c)

46. Philosophy means:
    (a) Love of wisdom
    (b) Love without wisdom
    (c) Love of Society
    (d) None of the above
47. Philosophy is the apex of the pyramid of knowledge.
    (a) True (b) False
48. Who is the author of *Advances of Learning*?
    (a) Socrates (b) Plato
    (c) Peter Louis (d) Francis Bacon
49. "Social Sciences are concerned with the laws that given society and social development of man" said by:
    (a) Aristotle (b) Socrates
    (c) Peter Louis (d) Charles Darwin
50. The author of the book *Social Contract* is:
    (a) Peter Louis (b) A.L. Edward
    (c) J.J. Rousseau (d) Francis Bacon
51. The year of establishment of 'Asiatic Society of Calcutta' is:
    (a) 1684 (b) 1912
    (c) 1884 (d) 1784
52. Cluster was formerly known as Subject Bundle.
    (a) True (b) False
53. "Historical research is the application of the scientific method of inquiry to historical problems" said by:
    (a) A.J. Wood (b) J.B. Best
    (c) Mouley (d) W.H. George
54. Who define that "Historical method of research is a system or right procedure for attainment of historical truth"?

Answer

46. (a) 47. (a) 48. (d) 49. (c) 50. (d)
51. (c) 52. (a) 53. (b)

(a) Allen Kent (b) Alan Pritchard
(c) Calvin Mooers (d) Richard F. Clark

55. 'Man is mortal, Shyam is a man, Shyam is mortal' this is an example of:
(a) Deductive reasoning (b) Seminal research
(c) Deduction (d) Historical research

56. Bradford's law and Zipf's law are used as:
(a) Citation analysis
(b) Rank frequency analysis data
(c) System analysis
(d) None of these

57. Agglomeration was formerly known as:
(a) Dissection (b) Cluster
(c) Subject Bundle (d) Partial Comprehension

58. Who gives rise to formation of Compound Subject?
(a) Lamination (b) Fusion
(c) Fission (d) Cluster

59. According to Dr. S.R. Ranganathan, "When the basic layer is basic subject and the other layers are isolate idea, a .... subject is formed":
(a) Basic (b) Compound
(c) Complex (d) Pure

60. Statistics for lawyer refers to:
(a) General relation (b) Influence relation
(c) Bias relation (d) Tool relation

61. Match the following:
(1) Pure subject (i) Fusion
(2) Basic subject (ii) Distillation
(3) Compound subject (iii) Loose Assemblage
(4) Complex subject (iv) Lamination

Answer

54. (d) 55. a) 56. (b) 57. (d) 58. (a)
59. (b) 60. (c)

Codes:

(a) 1(i), 2(ii), 3(iii), 4(iv) (b) 1(ii), 2(i), 3(iv), 4(iii)
(c) 1(i), 2(ii), 3(iv), 4(iii) (d) 1(ii), 2(i), 3(iii), 4(iv)

62. What is the process of division or breakup into parts:
(a) Dissection (b) Denudation
(c) Fission (d) Fusion

63. 'Agriculture of wheat' is an example of:
(a) Compound subject (b) Primary Basic subject
(c) Pure subject (d) Complex subject

64. 'Cataloguing in libraries' is an example of:
(a) Basic subject (b) Compound subject
(c) Complex subject (d) Primary Basic subject

65. 'Urban Female' is an example of:
(a) Pure subject (b) Compound subject
(c) Complex subject (d) Basic subject

66. What is the process of collecting together of entities into larger masses without cohesion among the components?
(a) Lamination (b) Fusion
(c) Fission (d) Agglomeration

67. 'Political Science' is:
(a) Basic subject (b) Primary Basic subject
(c) Compound subject (d) Complex subject

68. Nipponology is an example of:
(a) Lamination (b) Distillation
(c) Agglomeration (d) Cluster

69. Statistical Analysis is an example of:
(a) Dissection (b) Denudation
(c) Distillation (d) Lamination

Answer

61. (b) 62. (c) 63. (a) 64. (b) 65. (b)
66. (d) 67. (a) 68. (d) 69. (c)

70. Subject is a systematic and organized body of ideas.
    (a) True (b) False
71. The famous book *Das Capital* is written by:
    (a) Aristotle (b) Karl Marx
    (c) Max Weber (d) Francis Bacon
72. Who is the author of 'City of God':
    (a) Margaret Mann (b) Socrates
    (c) Donkar Deyvis (d) Thomas Acquinas
73. Theory of Evolution was first propounded by:
    (a) B. Lemare (b) C. Shannan
    (c) Karl Marx (d) Max Weber
74. The word 'Bibliomatrics' was first used by Allan Pritchard in the year 1969.
    (a) True (b) False
75. 'Bibliomatrics' is a study of:
    (a) Bibliotherapy
    (b) Bio-technology
    (c) Mathematics for librarianship
    (d) Mathematics for Bio-physics
76. Which of the following techniques employed in Bibliomatrics:
    (a) Counting
    (b) Citation analysis
    (c) Rank and size frequency distribution
    (d) All the above
77. Match the following:
    (1) History (i) Fusion
    (2) Indology (ii) Cluster
    (3) Bio-physics (iii) Agglomeration
    (4) Natural Sciences (iv) Distillation

Answer

70. (a) 71. (b) 72. (d) 73. (a) 74. (a)
75. (c) 76. (d)

Codes:

(a) 1(i), 2(ii), 3(iii), 4(iv)
(b) 1(iv), 2(ii), 3(i), 4(iii)
(c) 1(ii), 2(iii), 3(i), 4(iv)
(d) 1(iii), 2(ii), 3(i), 4(iv)

78. Law of sampling is related with:
 (a) Law of statistical regularity
 (b) Law of India
 (c) Both (a) and (b)
 (d) Neither (a) nor (b)

79. Law of Scattering is described by:
 (a) Bradford (b) G.K. Zipf
 (c) A.J. Lotka (d) Claudes Sharman

80. INFORSS stand for:
 (a) Information Retrieval System
 (b) Information Requirement of Social Sciences
 (c) Information Retrieval System for Social Sciences
 (d) Information Requirement for Sciences

81. INFORSS is one of the major user's studies conducted in UK.
 (a) True (b) False

82. Cranfield Tests was described by:
 (a) C.W. Cleverdon (b) Fermont Rider
 (c) G.K. Zipf (d) A.J. Lotka

83. Bio-technology is an example of:
 (a) Lamination (b) Dissection
 (c) Fission (d) Fusion

84. Match the following:
 (1) Authority centered thinking (i) Max Weber

Answer

77. (b) 78. (c) 79. (a) 80. (b) 81. (a)
82. (a) 83. (d)

(2) Positivistic thinking (ii) Aristotle
(3) Speculative thinking (iii) August Compte

Codes:

(a) 1(i), 2(ii), 3(iii) (b) 1(i), 2(iii), 3(ii)
(c) 1(ii), 2(iii), 3(i) (d) 1(ii), 2(i), 3(iii)

85. The bibliographical and type studies carried out in:
(a) Cranfield test (b) Case study
(c) Historical studies (d) Four cell studies

86. Match the following:
(1) Management (i) Agglomeration
(2) Humanities (ii) Cluster
(3) Oceanography (iii) Distillation
(4) Astrophysics (iv) Fusion

Codes:

(a) 1(i), 2(iii), 3(ii), 4(iv)
(b) 1(iii), 2(i), 3(ii), 4(iv)
(c) 1(iii), 2(iv), 3(ii), 4(i)
(d) 1(i), 2(ii), 3(iii), 4(iv)

87. 'Tree of porphyry' is formed as result of Dichotomy.
(a) True (b) False

88. Which of the following is the characteristic of hypothesis:
(a) Should be tested
(b) Should be economic
(c) Should be conceptual
(d) All the above

89. Which of the following is the function of hypothesis:
(a) Help in theory construction
(b) As a source of methodology
(c) As an organization principle
(d) All the above

Answer

84. (a) 85. (b) 86. (b) 87. (a) 88. (d)
89. (b)

90. 'Earth is round', it is an example of:
    (a) Conceptual hypothesis
    (b) Universal hypothesis
    (c) Experimental hypothcsis
    (d) Non-experimental hypothesis
91. The study of past is related to:
    (a) Experimental method of research
    (b) Survey method of research
    (c) Historical method of research
    (d) Spiral of scientific research
92. 'Grey Literature' means:
    (a) Literature which is semi-published
    (b) Literature which is to be published in future
    (c) Documents which are bound in grey cloth
    (d) Literature which contains classified information
93. Flow of information goes from:
    (a) Bottom to top (b) Top to bottom
    (c) Middle to bottom (d) Middle to top
94. The term 'Truncation' is used in:
    (a) Coordination (b) Budgeting
    (c) Search formulation (d) Thesaurus
95. The basic communication model was developed by:
    (a) Socrates (b) Plato
    (c) Charles Darwin (d) Aristotle
96. Knowledge is the organized form of information:
    (a) True (b) False
97. Indicate the name of the philosopher, who was the exponent of Scientific Method:
    (a) S.R. Ranganathan (b) Aristotle
    (c) F.W. Taylor (d) Bacon

Answer

90. (c) 91. (c) 92. (a) 93. (b) 94. (c)
95. (d) 96. (a) 97. (d)

98. A research proceeds from general to specific is:
    (a) Inductive logic (b) Deductive logic
    (c) Both (a) and (b) (d) None of the above

99. A research proceeds from specific to general is:
    (a) Inductive logic (b) Deductive logic
    (c) Both (a) and (b) (d) None of the above

100. Observation method is not used in:
    (a) Case study (b) Quantitative research
    (c) Conceptual research (d) Historical research

101. The questions, whose answers are already quoted to be chosen, are called:
    (a) Open ended questions
    (b) Close ended questions
    (c) Procoded
    (d) None of these

102. DISISS stands for:
    (a) Information Services in Social Sciences
    (b) Design of Information Service in the Social Sciences
    (c) Defence Information Service
    (d) None of these

103. Four important techniques used in explore the information need of users are:
    (a) Report, Questionnaire, Investigation, Observation
    (b) Dairy, Questionnaire, Investigation, Observation
    (c) Dairy, Questionnaire, Interview, Observation
    (d) None of the above

104. Which is the following research method is useful in a study on measuring the active life of periodicals:
    (a) Case Study (b) Interview
    (c) Survey (d) Citation analysis

Answer

98. (b) 99. (a) 100. (d) 101. (c) 102. (a)
103. (c) 104. (c)

105. 'Decachotomy' refers to a division into:
   (a) 2 (b) 10
   (c) 100 (d) None of these

106. 'Dichotomy' refers to a division into:
   (a) 2 (b) 10
   (c) 100 (d) Many

107. 'Polychotomy' refers to a division into:
   (a) 2 (b) 10
   (c) 100 (d) Many

108. In a research report/paper to refer to an immediate reference, the following term is used:
   (a) Ibid (b) Op. cit
   (c) Loc. cit (d) None of these

109. In a research report/paper to refer to an earlier but not immediately preceding reference, the term used:
   (a) Ibid (b) Op. cit
   (c) Loc. cit (d) None of these

110. "Knowledge in the modern information age is the central capital, the cost centre and the crucial resources of the economy" said by:
   (a) J.H. Shera (b) S.R. Ranganathan
   (c) Peter Drucker (d) H.E. Bliss

111. Inkblot test is developed by:
   (a) L. Guttman (b) Pritchard
   (c) Allen Kent (d) H. Rorschach

112. Which of the following method of research and useful study on measuring the action life periodical:
   (a) Cluster sampling (b) Citation analysis
   (c) Experiment (d) Survey

Answer

105. (b) 106. (a) 107. (d) 108. (a) 109. (b)
110. (c) 111. (d) 112. (b)

113. Conversion of Response into a set of number is called:
   (a) Coding (b) Cataloguing
   (c) Classification (d) Number setting

114. A footnote is:
   (a) A supplementary information to text
   (b) A bibliographical reference
   (c) Both (a) and (b)
   (d) None of the above

115. Mean, Median and Modes are measures of central tendency.
   (a) True (b) False

116. Research report is an account of:
   (a) Only conclusion
   (b) Only suggestion
   (c) Data analysis
   (d) Research work with conclusion and information

117. Result 30 items out of 60 is a .... statistics:
   (a) Sampling (b) Inferential
   (c) Descriptive (d) Time series

118. A systematic organization of data in column and rows is called:
   (a) Coding (b) Graphs
   (c) Data collection (d) Tabulation

119. Diagrams and graphs were used in statistic first by .... fair in 1762:
   (a) William Play (b) A. Pritchard
   (c) Kautilya (d) M. Weber

120. Spiral means:
   (a) Research process (b) A research tool
   (c) A process (d) An unending circle

Answer

113. (a) 114. (c) 115. (a) 116. (d) 117. (b)
118. (d) 119. (a) 120. (d)

121. The study aimed at finding out best method of charging of book is:
   (a) Relay research (b) Applied research
   (c) Experimental research (d) Basic research

122. A research design should not include:
   (a) Hypothesis (b) Methodology
   (c) Findings (d) Scope

123. Bibliographic coupling is a:
   (a) Identification of document
   (b) Technique for identify theme of document from its citation
   (c) Identification of author of document
   (d) None of the above

124. Scalogram Analysis was devised by:
   (a) Bogardus (b) Eckhendt
   (c) Plato (d) Louis Guttman

125. Systematic sampling is also known as:
   (a) Interval sampling (b) Cluster sampling
   (c) Random sampling (d) Stratified sampling

126. The book 'Motivation Factor a Theory of Personnel Management' is authored by:
   (a) Max Weber & A. Hezberg
   (b) Martin & Lorry A. Bruskemp
   (c) Peter Drucker & M. Weber
   (d) P. Drucker & Martin

127. During Vedic Period, Universe of knowledge is divided into:
   (a) Dharma, Darshan, Kama and Sahitya
   (b) Dharma, Kama, Darshan and Moksha
   (c) Dharma, Karma, Kama and Moksha
   (d) Dharma, Karma, Darshan and Moksha

Answer

121. (b) 122. (c) 123. (b) 124. (d) 125. (a)
126. (b) 127. (c)

128. A subject without any isolate idea:
    (a) Generic subject (b) Complex subject
    (c) Compound subject (d) Basic subject

129. The ability to successfully cope with one's own emotions and those others is known as
    (a) Theory of mind
    (b) Internal working model
    (c) Emotional competence
    (d) Strange situation

130. Reaction formation refers to the behaviour of a person who is trying toward off anxiety-causing and unacceptable impulses. To do this the person
    (a) will often stutter
    (b) will speak out against the behaviour which he himself is trying to suppress and will usually overemphasize his opinion
    (c) will make excuses for his behaviour
    (d) none of the above

131. Conservation refers to—
    (a) The appreciation that certain properties of an object remain constant despite some perceptual changes in the object
    (b) The belief that the height of a column of liquid is the sole determinant of the liquid's total volume
    (c) The fact that the preoperational child is incapable of performing certain perceptual transformation in his head
    (d) The fact that preoperational children preserve thoughts about other people

132. Dr. White's research shows that children born into the same family less than three years apart can be extremely difficult for parents to deal with: Why do you think this happens?

Answer

128. (d) 129. (c) 130 (c) 131. (a)

(a) Children who are close in age always pick on one another
(b) Because the mother has twin children, she is not sure which one to look after first and this frustrate both siblings
(c) Mothers always favour one child over the other, so one child always causes problems in order to get attention
(d) The older child resents the younger child and picks on him or her. As they grow, the younger child creates problems for the older child. There are ongoing battles which the parents must deal with

133. Which of the following is not a stage of risk management principles?
(a) Hazard control (b) Hazard maintenance
(c) Hazard assessment (d) Evaluation/monitoring

134. Principles of Design are:
(a) 4 (b) 3
(c) 2 (d) 5

135. Imaginative thinking occur at the age of:
(a) 3 years (b) 6 years
(c) 9 years (d) 12 years

136. We lose about a pint of water each day just by:
(a) breathing (b) sweating
(c) urinating (d) exercising

137. More than two groups are required to study the cause and effect relationship in the research design
(a) Ex-post facto (b) Survey
(c) Experimental (d) Exploratory

138. Which one of the following is non-probability sampling technique?

Answer

132. (d) 133. (c) 134. (d) 135. (d) 136. (b)
137. (a)

(a) Systematic random sampling
(b) Cluster sampling
(c) Snowball sampling
(d) Simple random sampling

139. Match the symbols of process chart (List I) with operations (List II):

List I (Symbols)		List II (Operations)
A. o	(i)	Movement and operation done simultaneously
B. O	(ii)	Movement from place to place
C. □	(iii)	Operation
D. ©	(iv)	Inspection for quality and quantity

Codes:	A	B	C	D
(a)	(i)	(iv)	(iii)	(ii)
(b)	(ii)	(i)	(iv)	(iii)
(c)	(iii)	(i)	(iv)	(ii)
(d)	(ii)	(iii)	(iv)	(i)

140. Match the method of research tools from List I to List II:

List I	List II
A. a document that contains a set of questions	(i) Interview
B. a set of structured questions in which answers are recorded by the researcher	(ii) Observation
C. a planned methodical watching the subject or situation	(iii) Questionnaire
D. an indirect technique of questioning about a task or situation	(iv) Projective

Codes:	A	B	C	D
(a)	(i)	(iv)	(iii)	(ii)
(b)	(ii)	(i)	(iv)	(iii)

Answer

138. (c) 139. (d)

(c)	(iii)	(i)	(iv)	(ii)
(d)	(i)	(iv)	(iii)	(ii)

141. A fixed curriculum for teaching is followed in:
   (a) Extension Education
   (b) Non-formal Education
   (c) Informal Education
   (d) Formal Education

142. In 'ex ante' evaluation a project is assessed:
   (a) After the project is completed
   (b) Before the project is executed
   (c) While the project is ongoing
   (d) Before and after the project is implemented

143. **Assertion (A):** Pre-testing of a tool of research is essential to carry out sound research.

   Reason (R): Vague and unclear/difficult questions can be modified or replaced.
   (a) Both (A) and (R) are true
   (b) (A) is true but (R) is false
   (c) (A) is false but (R) is true
   (d) Both (A) and (R) are false

144. **Assertion (A):** Retention of learning is more when variety of learning experiences are provided by the teacher.

   Reason (R): Retention is facilitated when two or more senses are used at a time of learning.
   (a) Both (A) and (R) are true
   (b) (A) is true but (R) is false
   (c) (A) is false but (R) is true
   (d) Both (A) and (R) are false

145. Match the items in List I with List II:

List I	**List II**
A. The values of variables are presented in vertical bars	(i) Line graph

Answer

140. (d) 141 (d) 142. (d) 143. (c) 144. (a)

B. The points are plotted and joined with each other	(ii) Bar diagram
C. Consists of many levels and presents one or two variables	(iii) Histogram
D. Consists of bars drawn either vertically or horizontally	(iv) Pyramid

Codes:	A	B	C	D
(a)	(i)	(iv)	(iii)	(ii)
(b)	(iii)	(i)	(iv)	(ii)
(c)	(i)	(ii)	(iv)	(iii)
(d)	(iii)	(i)	(ii)	(iv)

146. Bundura's social-cognitive learning asserts:
   (a) Learning specific observable responses
   (b) Cognitive thinking and problem-solving
   (c) Cognitive problem-solving skills and capacities
   (d) Learning behaviour, cognitive response pattern's social roles

147. Randomization model in research design is:
   (a) randomly dividing the sample in two or more groups
   (b) selecting random sample from population
   (c) selecting cluster as a sample
   (d) selecting available sample

148. A variable that can be manipulated is:
   (a) Continuous variable (b) Dependent variable
   (c) Independent variable (d) Discreet variable

149. An open-ended question elicits:
   (a) True data (b) Varied responses
   (c) Objective results (d) Leading answers

150. Arrange the following teaching learning methods in order of learner's ability:

Answer

145. (b) 146. (d) 147. (b) 148. (c) 149. (b)

(i) A video show (ii) Laboratory method
(iii) Demonstration (iv) Radio talk

Codes:

(a) (ii), (i), (iii), (iv) (b) (iv), (i), (iii), (ii)
(c) (i), (ii), (iii), (iv) (d) (ii), (iii), (i), (iv)

151. Arrange the steps of counselling process in right sequence:

1. Synthesis 2. Diagnosis
3. Analysis 4. Treatment and counselling
5. Follow up 6. Prognosis

Codes:

(a) 1,3,4,6,2 and 5 (b) 3,2,6,4,5 and 1
(c) 4,1,2,3,5 and 6 (d) 3,1,2,6,4 and 5

152. Arrange the following steps in research in the correct sequence:

(i) Sample Selection (ii) Research Question
(iii) Data Collection (iv) Research Design
(v) Objectives

Codes:

(a) (ii), (i), (iii), (iv), (v)
(b) (iv), (i), (iii), (ii), (v)
(c) (ii), (v), (i), (iv), (iii)
(d) (ii), (iii), (i), (iv), (v)

153. The following measure of Central Tendency and Dispersion are used in ANOVA:

(a) Mean and Standard Deviation
(b) Mean and Variance
(c) Mean and Standard Error
(d) Median and Standard Deviation

154. The correlation between two variables is said to be perfectly positive if the value is equal to:

Answer

150. (b) 151. (a) 152. (c) 153. (b)

(a) 0 (b) −1
(c) +1 (d) 0.1

155. Match the following:

List I	List II
A. Histogram	(i) Dispersion
B. Mean	(ii) Ordinal scale
C. Standard deviation	(iii) Central tendency
D. Qualitative variable	(iv) Graphical Representation of frequency distribution

Codes:	A	B	C	D
(a)	(i)	(iv)	(iii)	(ii)
(b)	(ii)	(i)	(iv)	(iii)
(c)	(iv)	(i)	(iii)	(ii)
(d)	(iv)	(iii)	(i)	(ii)

156. Give the correct sequence in writing a Research Proposal:

(i) Review of literature (ii) Introduction
(iii) Bibliography (iv) Objectives
(v) Methodology (vi) Analysis of data

Codes:

(a)	(i)	(iv)	(iii)	(ii)	(v)	(vi)
(b)	(ii)	(i)	(iv)	(iii)	(vi)	(v)
(c)	(iv)	(i)	(ii)	(iii)	(v)	(vi)
(d)	(iv)	(ii)	(i)	(v)	(vi)	(iii)

157. The researcher lives with the cultural community for a period of months or years is known as:

(a) Clinical study (b) Case study
(c) Specimen record (d) Ethnography

158. Write the correct sequence of the steps in data analysis:

(i) Data entry (ii) Statistical treatment
(iii) Coding (iv) Tabulation

Answer

154. (c) 155. (d) 156. (d) 157. (b)

Codes:

(a) (i), (iii), (iv), (ii) (b) (iv), (iii), (ii), (i)
(c) (iii), (ii), (i), (iv) (d) (iii), (iv), (ii), (i)

159. Match the statistical test (List I) with given description (List II):

List I	List II
A. Correlation	(i) Comparison of means of more than two groups
B. Chi-square	(ii) Comparison of pre- and post-testing mean scores of a sample
C. Paired t-test	(iii) Strength and direction of relationship between two variables
D. Duncan test	(iv) Data is in frequencies

Codes:	A	B	C	D
(a)	(iii)	(iv)	(ii)	(i)
(b)	(ii)	(i)	(iv)	(iii)
(c)	(iv)	(i)	(iii)	(ii)
(d)	(iii)	(i)	(ii)	(iv)

160. Type I error is committed, when:
    (a) Null hypothesis is true, and it is rejected
    (b) Null Hypothesis is true, and it is accepted
    (c) Null Hypothesis is false, and it is accepted
    (d) Null Hypothesis is false, and it is rejected

161. A researcher wishing to graphically represent the Infant Mortality Rate in different States of India would do it by:
    (a) Histogram (b) Bar Diagramme
    (c) Pie Chart (d) Frequency Curve

162. Write the correct sequence of the steps in data analysis:
    (i) Data entry (ii) Interpretation
    (iii) Coding (iv) Tabulation

Answer

158. (a) 159. (a) 160. (c) 161. (a)

Codes:

(a) (i), (iii), (iv), (ii) (b) (iv), (iii), (ii), (i)
(c) (iii), (ii), (i), (iv) (d) (iii), (iv), (ii), (i)

163. Students arrange books on their desk in an order as per subjects in Time Table is:
   (a) Change in hand and body motion
   (b) Change in work, storage space and equipment
   (c) Change in production process
   (d) Change in raw materials

164. Which one of the following is a non-probability sampling technique?
   (a) Random sampling
   (b) Snowball sampling
   (c) Systemic random sampling
   (d) Cluster sampling

165. Identify the statement giving the correct sequence of steps in data analysis:
   (a) Coding, tabulation, data entry, interpretation
   (b) Coding, data entry, tabulation, interpretation
   (c) Interpretation, tabulation, coding, data entry
   (d) Tabulation, coding, data entry, interpretation

166. Type I error is made when:
   (a) True null hypothesis is rejected
   (b) True null hypothesis is accepted
   (c) False null hypothesis is rejected
   (d) False null hypothesis is accepted

167. The variance is:
   (i) Directly proportional to the average squared difference between all pairs of observations
   (ii) Smallest when calculated from the mean
   (iii) Denoted by symbol Ó
   (iv) Described as the dispersion of the distribution

Answer

162. (a) 163. (b) 164. (b) 165. (b) 166. (a)

Codes:

(a) (i) and (iii) are correct
(b) (ii) and (iii) are correct
(c) (i), (ii and (iii) are correct
(d) (i), (ii and (iv) are correct

168. **Assertion (A):** The existence of a correlation between two variables can be shown to exist only when there is variability.

Reason (R): If one of the variables is a constant, with no variability, then the correlation coefficient is not even defined.

(a) (A) is true but (R) is false
(b) (A) is false but (R) is true
(c) Both (A) and (R) are true and (R) is the correct explanation
(d) Both (A) and (R) are false

169. Arrange the correct order of steps in research:

(i) Review of literature (ii) Objectives
(iii) Rationale (iv) Methodology
(v) Interpretation (vi) Results

Codes:

(a) (v), (iv), (vi), (ii), (i), (iii)
(b) (ii), (i), (iv), (iii), (v), (vi)
(c) (iii), (iv), (i), (ii), (vi), (v)
(d) (iii), (ii), (i), (iv), (vi), (v)

170. Mrs Khurana wants to teach her preschool class not to fight toys. What does your knowledge suggests as a good method?

(a) Show the children alternatives to aggressive behaviour
(b) Make sure she has only one toy to each type for every child

Answer

167. (d) 168. (b) 169. (a)

(c) Punish the grabbing behaviour
(d) Ignore the aggression

171. F-test is used:
   (a) To make an estimate of the population
   (b) To design a randomization model
   (c) To text the difference between means of two or more groups
   (d) To check the design of experiment

172. Which of the following scale is 'summated rating scale' used to measure attitude?
   (a) Likert's scale
   (b) Bongardus scale
   (c) Thurstone scale
   (d) Guttman's scale

173. From which plant source gluten is derived?
   (a) Soya
   (b) Wheat
   (c) Rice
   (d) Corn

174. Chi-square test is used:
   (a) When there are only two groups for comparison
   (b) When the data is in frequencies
   (c) To check accuracy of data
   (d) When there are three or more groups for comparison

175. An example of cross-sectional study is:
   (a) Comparing individuals of various ages at the same time
   (b) Continued observations of the same individuals
   (c) Careful description by the researcher
   (d) One that requires no manipulation

176. The most appropriate statistical test for analysing quantitative data is:
   (a) Median test
   (b) Sign test
   (c) t-test
   (d) Chi-square

Answer

170. (b) 171. (a) 172. (a) 173. (b) 174. (b)
175. (a) 176. (d)

177. Two variables are said to be positively correlated if—
   (a) the change in one variable results in a corresponding change in the other variable
   (b) the change of the variables is the opposite directions
   (c) the two variables are similar in nature
   (d) the two variables are dissimilar

178. Which of the following method is used to test reliability of a measurement instrument?
   (a) Split half (b) Interview
   (c) Test retest (d) Observation

179. A predictive statement that relates an independent variable to a dependent variable:
   (a) Objective (b) Hypothesis
   (c) Extraneous variable (d) Psychological variable

180. A portion of output reentered as input to affect succeeding output is:
   (a) Feedback (b) Deferred resource
   (c) Throughput (d) Black box

181. **Assertion (A):** The research study must start with the formulation of hypothesis.

   Reason (R): Hypothesis will help to extrapolate the sample results to the population.
   (a) (A) is true but (R) is false
   (b) (A) is false but (R) is true
   (c) Both (A) and (R) are true
   (d) Both (A) and (R) are false

182. Write the correct sequence in writing a research article:
   (i) Review of literature (ii) Bibliography
   (iii) Introduction (iv) Methodology
   (v) Objectives (vi) Results and conclusion

Answer

177. (c) 178. (a) 179. (b) 180. (a) 181. (b)

Codes:

(a) (iii), (v), (i), (iv), (vi), (ii)
(b) (iv), (i), (vi), (ii), (iii), (v)
(c) (iii), (iv), (i), (ii), (vi), (v)
(d) (i), (iii), (ii), (iv), (v), (vi)

183. Match the statistical test in List I with the description in List II:

List I	List II
A. t-test	(i) testing difference in means of more than two groups
B. F-test	(ii) data is in frequencies
C. Chi-square	(iii) bivariate distribution
D. Pearson's	(iv) testing mean against population mean

Codes:	A	B	C	D
(a)	(iii)	(iv)	(i)	(ii)
(b)	(ii)	(i)	(iv)	(iii)
(c)	(iv)	(i)	(iii)	(ii)
(d)	(iv)	(iii)	(ii)	(i)

184. Which one of the following pairs is not correctly matched?
   (a) An in-depth study of a person is referred to as analytical study.
   (b) In questionnaire in a logical sequence from easy to move difficult questions.
   (c) Rorschach test consists of ten card having prints of ink blots.
   (d) Quizzes and tests are used to assess the memorising and analytical ability of respondents.

185. **Assertion (A):** Critical analysis of a research report is valuable for researcher.

Reason (R): Through a critical analysis the researcher gains some insight into the nature of a researcher problem,

Answer

182. (a) 183. (d) 184. (a)

methods used and conclusions drawn.

(a) (A) is true but (R) is false
(b) (A) is false but (R) is true
(c) Both (A) and (R) are true
(d) Both (A) and (R) are false

186. The most appropriate statistical test for analysis qualitative data is:

(i) Pearson's r (ii) Sign test
(iii) Kruskal-Wallis test (iv) F-test

Codes:

(a) (i) and (ii) are correct
(b) (ii) and (iii) are correct
(c) (i) and (iii) are correct
(d) (ii), (iii) and (iv) are correct

Answer

185. (b) 186. (c)

Chapter 5

Institutional Management

1. Group care is best for babies because—
   (a) They will learn to share
   (b) One person can easily look after three babies at once
   (c) The babies will learn to speak more quickly
   (d) None of the above
2. What characterizes the interactionist approach to language acquisition?
   (a) Language is an interaction between speaker and listener
   (b) Language is the link between what you think and what you do
   (c) There is a link between the environmental and biological factors in the process of acquiring language
   (d) There is a link among different languages
3. What are we led to believe is the source of happiness in a consumer society?
   (a) Buying new things (b) Friends
   (c) Community (d) Family
4. Duty of care means:
   (a) Accepting responsibility for other people's mistakes
   (b) Giving out advice and relevant accident forms to injured members

Answer

1. (a) 2. (a) 3. (a)

(c) Having a working knowledge of rules
(d) Accepting responsibility for health and safety in workplace

5. Some babies who are just beginning to develop emotional attachments and some degree of communication have a difficult time with strangers. Why is this?
(a) The stranger may not hold the baby properly
(b) The stranger may miss subtle cues from the baby and then not meet the baby's expectations. This may confuse the baby
(c) The stranger may look like someone the baby does not like
(d) The stranger's voice may be upsetting to the baby

6. The ability to successfully cope with one's own emotions and those others is known as
(a) Theory of mind
(b) Internal working model
(c) Emotional competence
(d) Strange situation

7. Conservation refers to
(a) The appreciation that certain properties of an object remain constant despite some perceptual changes in the object
(b) The belief that the height of a column of liquid is the sole determinant of the liquid's total volume
(c) The fact that the preoperational child is incapable of performing certain perceptual transformation in his head
(d) The fact that preoperational children preserve thoughts about other people

8. Which statement is false?
(a) Vertigo can occur in children as young as 18 months
(b) Vertigo attacks may last anywhere from a few minutes to several days

Answer

4. (d) 5. (b) 6. (c) 7. (a)

(c) Vertigo can be very uncomfortable, but never life-threatening
(d) Benign positional vertigo is common among older people

9. According to UN studies:
(a) The vast majority of the world's young people have no idea how HIV is transmitted
(b) The vast majority of the world's young people have no idea how to protect themselves
(c) Adolescence is the time when the majority of people become sexually active and the tragic consequence is that they fall prey to HIV
(d) (a), (b) and (c)

10. What is meant by the term "ghosts in the nursery"?
(a) Some parents used to tell ghost stories to children when they went to bed
(b) Most children pretend they see ghosts in their room at night so that their parents will come back into their room several times
(c) Most of the time ghosts appear in a nursery
(d) It refers to the thoughts and feelings that are buried deep in our minds since childhood which affect how we deal with others

11. Which one of the following is most distinctively a trait?
(a) Ecstasy (b) Trustfulness
(c) Anger (d) Happiness

12. What is health economics?
(a) A study of cost containment
(b) A study of resource allocation
(c) A study of optimal resource allocation
(d) Traditional economics applied on health care

Answer

8. (a) 9. (d) 10. (d) 11. (b) 12. (c)

13. Flow can the findings of health economics be used?
    (a) To determine which services to provide
    (b) To determine who should get the services provided
    (c) To determine where and how to provide services
    (d) All of the above
14. What is derived demand?
    (a) The demand for health
    (b) The demand for health care
    (c) The demand expressed by a health professional
    (d) The demand motivated by a health professional
15. What is information asymmetry and why does it restrict consumer sovereignty?
    (a) Health providers possess more knowledge than consumers
    (b) Health professionals do not inform patients
    (c) Patients have no power in the health care market
    (d) Health providers cause a level of consumption higher than patients would have chosen
16. What is a photic sneezer?
    (a) Someone who sneezes at will
    (b) Someone who sneezes when being photographed
    (c) Someone who sneezes when exposed to bright light
    (d) Someone who sneezes when pinched
17. Which of the following is not a defense mechanism?
    (a) Denial (b) Reality principle
    (c) Reaction formation (d) Projection
18. The World Health Organization says formula feeding is the
    (a) First best choice for babies
    (b) Second best choice for babies

Answer

13. (d) 14. (d) 15. (d) 16. (c) 17. (b)

(c) Third best choice for babies
(d) Fourth best choice for babies

19. How long is breast feeding recommended by the American Academy of Pediatrics?
(a) Three months (b) Six months
(c) Nine months (d) Twelve months

20. A baby is the safest when it sleeps:
(a) In a room by itself
(b) In a room with another young child
(c) With its parents
(d) In a room with the family dog

21. If all babies slept with their parents, which of the following would happen?
(a) The crib manufacturers would lose money
(b) The manufacturers of Queen and King size beds would make more money
(c) There would be more happy babies
(d) All the above

22. HIV/AIDS has:
(a) No cure
(b) A treatment that delays the onset of AIDS, slows the progression of the disease and prolongs life
(c) A treatment that have some success preventing mother to child transmission
(d) (a), (b) and (c)

23. In countries where the spread of HIV/AIDS is slowing or declining, it is primarily because
(a) Young men and women are being given the knowledge to adopt safe behaviour
(b) Young men and women are being given the tools and services to adopt safe behaviour

Answer

18. (b) 19. (d) 20. (c) 21. (c) 22. (d)

(c) Young men and women are provided with protective environment to develop the skills necessary to avoid infection
(d) (a), (b) and (c)

24. What is the relationship between demand and need for health care?
(a) Need is always turned into demand
(b) Only normative need is turned into demand
(c) Only felt need is turned into demand
(d) Only expressed need is turned into demand

25. A mother can make the transition from her womb to the outside world easier for her baby by:
(a) Holding the baby close to her body
(b) Carrying the baby
(c) Sleeping with the baby
(d) All the above

26. How recent is the practice of carrying babies in a sling?
(a) It just started ten years ago
(b) Different societies have been doing it throughout history
(c) It began in Central Africa about two centuries ago
(d) It began about 500 years ago by North American Indians

27. The older sibling may be very upset and troubled after the newborn sibling has been in the home for six months or longer. What is a sign that this older sibling may be upset?
(a) The older sibling reverts to using a pacifier
(b) The older sibling has temper tantrums
(c) The older sibling who has been toilet trained goes back to wetting themselves
(d) Any or all of the above

Answer

23. (d) 24. (a) 25. (d) 26. (b) 27. (d)

28. What is meant by the term "defense mechanism"?
    (a) It refers, to the ways in which a parent can defend or protect a child in his younger years
    (b) It refers to things we do to deflect our thoughts or feelings away from situations or ideas that are uncomfortable for us
    (c) It refers to a part of the brain where a certain mechanism allows us to think clearly
    (d) It refers to people who have always been defensive because they are paranoid.

29. A child who is severely disciplined by the teacher at lunchtime then goes to the cafeteria and deliberately starts a fight with another student. What defense mechanism might the child be using?
    (a) Suppression (b) Denial
    (c) Displacement (d) Minimizing

30. Which of the following situations is an example of the defense mechanism called "diversion"?
    (a) A person who gets drunk everyday says they do not have a problem with alcohol
    (b) A person who fails in driver's exam says the examiner just didn't like him
    (c) When a wife asks her husband to talk about a problem they have been experiencing, he says that he has to go outside to water the lawn
    (d) None of the above

31. The limbic system is involved in
    (a) Motor control
    (b) Emotion and learning
    (c) Preparing the body for action
    (d) Sensory control

Answer

28. (b) 29. (c) 30. (c) 31. (b)

32. Which is the most common and effective approaches to child rearing in many ethnic groups and cultures?
    (a) Permissive child rearing
    (b) Authoritative child rearing
    (c) Authoritarian child rearing
    (d) Uninvolved child rearing
33. Which of the following is usually associated with internalizing problems?
    (a) Loneliness (b) Victimization
    (c) Anxiety (d) All of the above
34. What is a Freudian slip?
    (a) A nightdress
    (b) An expression of unconscious desire
    (c) A mistake made during analysis
    (d) An unconscious expression of a person stuck at the anal stage
35. A critical period for language acquisition refers to:
    (a) The period for transition between 1 and 2 word utterances
    (b) The time in one's childhood in which language must develop if it is to be fully learned
    (c) The period that isolated children spend by themselves before someone begins to teach them language
    (d) The period from 6-10 years of age during which certain complex aspects of syntax are learned
36. Which of the following oils is saturated fat (bad for your cholesterol count)?
    (a) Olive oil (b) Palm oil/coconut oil
    (c) Peanut oil (d) Olive oil/Canola oil
37. Women over 50 should consume
    (a) 1,500 milligrams of calcium/day
    (b) Six glasses of non-fat milk/day

Answer

32. (c) 33. (d) 34. (b) 35. (d) 36. (b)

(c) Three Tums/Oscal tablets/day
(d) Any of the above

38. Aerobic exercise must be sustained exercise (no stopping and starting) lasting at least
    (a) 5 minutes (b) 10 minutes
    (c) 20 minutes (d) 60 minutes

39. The major cause of chronic bad breath is
    (a) Creation of sulphur gases by bacteria which feed on residual food particles
    (b) Eating of foods like onions, cabbage, and garlic
    (c) Lack of fats in diet
    (d) The chemical interaction of food with certain salivary proteins

40. To which part of the term 'brachial' refer?
    (a) To the stomach (b) To the heart
    (c) To the arms (d) To the eyes

41. Which of the following may be the best way to help lower your risk of prostate cancer?
    (a) Take vitamin E supplements
    (b) Eat a healthy diet, rich with fruits, vegetables and whole grains
    (c) Drink green tea twice a day
    (d) Eat tomatoes or tomato products daily

42. Where in the body is the labyrinth?
    (a) Ear (b) Throat
    (c) Eye (d) Leg

43. What is Creatine Monohydrate?
    (a) Amino acid
    (b) Supplemental form of creatine
    (c) Vitamin D
    (d) Carbohydrates

Answer

37. (d) 38. (c) 39. (a) 40. (c) 41. (b)
42. (a) 43. (a)

44. What is Oleuropein?
    (a) Glycoside found in green olive leaves
    (b) An olive
    (c) Scientific name of the Green Olive Tree
    (d) None of these
45. What conditions can cause symptoms similar to Alzheimer's disease?
    (a) Parkinson's disease, Huntington's disease, brain tumour, head injury
    (b) Thyroid gland disorders, nutritional deficiencies, hormone or electrolyte imbalances
    (c) Medication side effects, drug interactions, alcoholism
    (d) Emotional trauma, clinical depression, schizophrenia, delirium
46. Treatments for gum is disease include:
    (a) Scaling and root planning
    (b) Regular flossing
    (c) Medication
    (d) (a) and (c)
47. When you check your moles for signs of cancer, what should you look for?
    (a) Changes to the mole's colour or shape
    (b) Oozing or seepage from the mole
    (c) Multiple hairs
    (d) A raised, ring-like marking on the mole's surface
48. What are chronic diseases?
    (a) Diseases you catch over and over
    (b) Antibiotic-resistant bacterial infections
    (c) Diseases that are not completely curable and don't go away on their own
    (d) Sexually transmitted diseases, like AIDS and herpes

Answer

44. (a) 45. (a) 46. (d) 47. (a) 48. (c)

49. What determines the flavour of honey?
    (a) The age of the bee
    (b) The pasteurizing technique
    (c) The celestial season
    (d) The type of flower from which it gathered

50. What is osteoporosis?
    (a) A disease marked by low bone mass and deteriorating structure of bone tissue
    (b) A complication of obesity where bones break easily under the strain of excess weight
    (c) A type of cancer that causes bones to shrink and a part
    (d) A hereditary condition characterized by short stature and small body frame

51. Which of these foods is not a good source of antioxidants?
    (a) Iceberg lettuce (b) Tea
    (c) Spinach (d) Carrots

52. Which of the following is not a part of environmental hygiene and keeping your place free from clutter or conditions that allow bacteria and vermin to thrive?
    (a) Follow correct storage and garbage removal procedures
    (b) Maintain and clean equipments at the highest standard of hygiene
    (c) Carry personal hygiene kits (bum bags) with gloves and mask
    (d) Wash your hands regularly

53. Which of the following is not a hazard that can cause injury or harm in your place?
    (a) Crowd control
    (b) Spills and slippery surfaces like water, food and oil

Answer

49. (d) 50. (a) 51. (a) 52. (d)

(c) Incorrect storage including flammable materials having special storage requirements
(d) Environmental conditions such as sun exposure

54. Which of the following is not a stage of risk management principles?
(a) Hazard control (b) Hazard maintenance
(c) Hazard assessment (d) Evaluation/monitoring

55. What do warts look like?
(a) Smooth, flat lesions the size of pinheads
(b) Rough and round lumps that are lighter in colour than surrounding skin
(c) Oval lumps that are darker than normal skin
(d) All of the above

56. One of the most important but often neglected aspects of first aid treatment is
(a) Calling for help (b) Reassuring the patient
(c) Checking for danger (d) Assessing the patient

57. Symptoms of a fracture
(a) pain and tenderness
(b) possible bleeding at wound site
(c) deformity and swelling at wound site
(d) possible discoloration

58. The most appropriate fluid to give to a conscious patient suffering from hypothermia is
(a) Cool freshwater
(b) Sweet carbonated drinks
(c) A small amount of alcohol
(d) Warm, sweet drinks

59. How is vertigo treated?
(a) No treatment is required (b) Medication
(c) Surgery (d) All of the above

Answer

53. (a) 54. (c) 55. (d) 56. (b) 57. (c)
58. (d) 59. (d)

60. pH 7 indicates that the solution or substance is—
    (a) Acidic (b) Alkaline
    (c) Neutral (d) Salty

61. Glycogen is stored in—
    (a) Liver (b) Muscle
    (c) Liver and muscle (d) Heart

62. Ascorbic acid is the name of vitamin—
    (a) A (b) B
    (c) C (d) D

63. The universal recipient blood group is—
    (a) A (b) B
    (c) AB (d) O

64. Which one of the following is not a good method of money investment?
    (a) FDR (b) LIC
    (c) NSC (d) Lottery

65. Blood vessels which bring blood to the heart are:
    (a) Arteries (b) Veins
    (c) Capillaries (d) Nerves

66. Removal of permanent hardness of water is done by:
    (a) By boiling
    (b) Clark's process
    (c) Adding caustic soda
    (d) Calgon process

67. Colon cancer occurs more commonly in:
    (a) Men (b) Women
    (c) Both men and women (d) None of these

68. What is not a risk factor of colon cancer?
    (a) High calcium intake (b) Smoking
    (c) High-fat diet (d) Sedentary lifestyle

Answer

60. (c) 61. (c) 62. (c) 63. (c) 64. (d)
65. (b) 66. (b) 67. (c) 68. (a)

69. Which sentence is true about varicose veins?
    (a) They can be treated with laser surgery
    (b) Obesity, menopause and ageing add to the problem
    (c) They occur when the valves in your veins malfunction
    (d) All of the above

70. Which is a home remedy for heartburn?
    (a) Swallowing a tea spoon of yellow mustard
    (b) Sleeping without a pillow
    (c) Drinking milk
    (d) Eating peppermint candy

71. Which of the following does not contain caffeine?
    (a) Excedrin tablets
    (b) Coffee-flavored ice cream
    (c) Decaffeinated coffee
    (d) Mug Root Beer

72. What is diabetes?
    (a) A disease in which the pancreas produces a toxic form of insulin
    (b) A disease in which the pancreas produces an insufficient amount of insulin or the body has a decreased ability to process insulin
    (c) A disease brought on by an abnormal flow of insulin to the pancreas rather than the kidneys
    (d) A disease in which the body abnormally rejects any form of sugar

73. What is not a risk factor of Type 2 diabetes?
    (a) Family history (b) Heavy alcohol use
    (c) High blood pressure (d) Diet

74. To prevent complications, people with diabetes should:
    (a) consult their eye doctor regularly
    (b) check their feet daily for any sores, changes or signs of infection

Answer

69. (b) 70. (c) 71. (c) 72. (b) 73. (d)

(c) brush and floss their teeth daily
(d) all of the above

75. Which type of headache commonly occurs in adolescents and adults of both sexes?
(a) Migraine
(b) Cluster headache
(c) Tension headache
(d) Unisex headache

76. Which statement is false?
(a) Cosmetic surgery may cause migraines
(b) Pain behind one eye is characteristic of a cluster headache
(c) Lowering blood pressure can reduce headaches
(d) Honey can prevent headaches from hangovers

77. What causes this condition?
(a) Stiff muscles
(b) Carrying large packages
(c) Repetitive wrist movement
(d) Heavy bracelets

78. What is carpal tunnel syndrome?
(a) A painful condition of the wrist caused by pressure on the nerve inside a tunnel-like passage
(b) Weak bones that form a tunnel in the wrist
(c) Overuse of the tunnel muscle in the hand
(d) Feeling claustrophobic in a carpool going through a tunnel

79. A cut/slice/chunk of pork must be cooked to an internal temperature of at least
(a) 130°F for at least 15 seconds
(b) 145°F for at least 15 seconds
(c) 155°F for at least 15 seconds
(d) 165°F for at least 15 seconds

Answer

74. (d) 75. (c) 76. (d) 77. (c) 78. (a)
79. (a)

80. How do we check for breathing?
    (a) Look, touch, feel
    (b) Look, listen, feel
    (c) Listen, look, touch
    (d) Touch, talk and listen
81. Which of the following is not a stage of risk management principles?
    (a) Hazard control (b) Hazard maintenance
    (c) Hazard assessment (d) Evaluation/monitoring
82. The best method of resolving the conflict is:
    (a) Dominance (b) Compromise
    (c) Conversion (d) Integration
83. Which one of the following is a principle of management
    (a) Hierarchy (b) Organising
    (c) Job description (d) Evaluation
84. **Assertion (A):** Brocade, Huckaback, Jacquard and Tapestry can be classified under the same category.

    Reason (R): All can be made on the Jacquard loom.
    (a) (A) is true but (R) is false
    (b) (A) is false but (R) is true
    (c) Both (A) and (R) are true
    (d) Both (A) and (R) are false
85. **Assertion (A):** A Management is an end in itself.

    Reason (R): Home management is a means to achieve family goals.
    (a) (A) is correct but (R) is false
    (b) (A) is false but (R) is correct
    (c) Both (A) and (R) are correct
    (d) Both (A) and (R) are false

Answer

80. (b) 81. (c) 82. (d) 83. (d) 84. (c)
85. (c)

86. **Assertion (A):** Time is the human resource.

Reason (R): Time is the easiest to be measured but one of the most difficult to understand.

(a) (A) is true but (R) is false
(b) (A) is false but (R) is true
(c) Both (A) and (R) are true
(d) Both (A) and (R) are false

87. **Assertion (A):** Altruism is selfish concern for the welfare of others.

Reason (R): Altruism acts are motivated by internalized values, goals and self rewards.

(a) (A) is true but (R) is false
(b) (A) is false but (R) is true
(c) Both (A) and (R) are true
(d) Both (A) and (R) are false

88. **Assertion (A):** Monitoring of a programme is essential for its successful completion.

Reason (R): Monitoring helps the progress of the programme from time to time.

(a) (A) is true but (R) is false
(b) (A) is false but (R) is true
(c) Both (A) and (R) are true
(d) Both (A) and (R) are false

89. **Assertion (A):** Three persons sitting at different places can have a common talk through audio/video conferencing.

Reason (R): Internet and electronic media facilitate the contact amongst different persons at a time.

(a) (A) is true but (R) is false
(b) (A) is false but (R) is true
(c) Both (A) and (R) are true
(d) Both (A) and (R) are false

Answer

86. (c) 87. (d) 88. (c) 89. (b)

90. Give the correct sequence of prosocial reasoning stages:
   (i) Hedonistic
   (ii) Recognition of needs of others
   (iii) Seeking other's approval and acceptance
   (iv) Empathic

   Codes:
   (a) (i), (ii), (iii), (iv)   (b) (ii), (iii), (iv), (i)
   (c) (ii), (i), (iii), (iv)   (d) (ii), (iii), (i), (iv)

91. Write the correct sequence of attachment process:
   (i) Pre-attachment
   (ii) Attachment-in-the-making
   (iii) clear-cut attachment
   (iv) Goal-corrected partnership

   Codes:
   (a) (i), (iv), (iii), (ii)   (b) (i), (ii), (iii), (iv)
   (c) (ii), (i), (iii), (iv)   (d) (ii), (iii), (i), (iv)

92. Write the sequence of programmes of rural development by the years of commencement
   (i) National Rural Employment Programme
   (ii) Food for Work Programme
   (iii) Development of Women and Children in Rural Areas
   (iv) Jawahar Gram Samridhi Yojana

   Codes:
   (a) (i), (ii), (iii), (iv)   (b) (i), (iii), (ii), (iv)
   (c) (ii), (i), (iii), (iv)   (d) (ii), (iii), (i), (iv)

93. Match the items in List I with List II:

List I	List II
A. William Perkins	(i) Research on fibre polymer
B. Nelly Sethna	(ii) Mercerization
C. Carother Brothers	(iii) Kalamkari
D. Lowe	(iv) Mauvine dye

Answer

90. (b)   91. (b)   92. (c)

Codes:	A	B	C	D
(a)	(i)	(iv)	(iii)	(ii)
(b)	(ii)	(i)	(iv)	(iii)
(c)	(iii)	(i)	(iv)	(ii)
(d)	(iv)	(iii)	(i)	(ii)

94. Match the theoretical concepts in List I with the name of the theorist List II:

List I

A. Theory of multiple intelligence
B. Preoperational stage
C. Chronosystem
D. Information processing theory

List II

(i) J. Piaget (ii) H. Gardner
(iii) U. Bronfenbrenner (iv) Sternberg

Codes:	A	B	C	D
(a)	(ii)	(i)	(iii)	(iv)
(b)	(ii)	(i)	(iv)	(iii)
(c)	(iii)	(i)	(iv)	(ii)
(d)	(iii)	(ii)	(i)	(iv)

95. FIFO System is used in:
(a) Dining room (b) Purchase
(c) Store (d) Menu planning

96. Which is not a human resource?
(a) Energy (b) Time
(c) Money (d) Knowledge

97. Evaluation of any development programme is done against:
(a) Desires (b) Cost
(c) Resources (d) Objectives

Answer

93. (d) 94. (a) 95. (c) 96. (c) 97. (d)

98. **Assertion (A):** Work simplification means, accomplishing more work within a given amount of time and energy.

Reason (R): Accomplishment work efficiently.

(a) (A) is true but (R) is false
(b) (A) is false but (R) is true
(c) Both (A) and (R) are true
(d) Both (A) and (R) are false

99. Give the right sequence of the following:

(i) DOPA (ii) Polyphenols
(iii) Orthoquinones (iv) Melanins

Codes:

(a) (i), (iv), (iii), (ii) (b) (i), (iii), (ii), (iv)
(c) (ii), (i), (iii), (iv) (d) (ii), (iii), (i), (iv)

100. Steps in making budget are:

(i) Bringing expected income and expenditure into balance
(ii) Estimate total expected income
(iii) Estimate coat of desired items
(iv) List commodities

Codes:

(a) (ii), (iii), (i), (iv) (b) (i), (ii), (iii), (iv)
(c) (ii), (i), (iii), (iv) (d) (ii), (iii), (iv), (i)

101. Identify the correct sequence of Case's stages of cognition:

(i) Sensory motor control structures
(ii) Relational control structures
(iii) Dimensional control structures
(iv) Abstract control structures

(a) (i), (iv), (ii), (iii) (b) (i), (iii), (ii), (iv)
(c) (ii), (i), (iii), (iv) (d) (ii), (iii), (i), (iv)

102. Identify the correct sequence of Selman's stages of perspective taking:

Answer

98. (c) 99. (b) 100. (a) 101. (a)

(i) Social-informational perspective taking
(ii) Self-reflective perspective taking
(iii) Third party perspective taking
(iv) Societal perspective taking

Codes:

(a) (ii), (iii), (iv), (i) (b) (i), (iii), (ii), (iv)
(c) (ii), (i), (iii), (iv) (d) (ii), (iii), (i), (iv)

103. Arrange the different types of objective tests according to the level of difficulty:

(i) Matching type tests
(ii) Completion-selection type
(iii) True / False
(iv) Multiple Choice

Codes:

(a) (i), (iv), (iii), (ii) (b) (ii), (iii), (i), (iv)
(c) (ii), (i), (iii), (iv) (d) (ii), (iii), (i), (iv)

104. Match the records given in List I with units of food service institutions given in List II:

List I	List II
A. Menu card	(i) Kitchen
B. Invoice	(ii) Store
C. Stock book	(iii) Purchase
D. KOT	(iv) Dining Room

Codes:	A	B	C	D
(a)	(i)	(iv)	(iii)	(ii)
(b)	(ii)	(i)	(iv)	(iii)
(c)	(iv)	(iii)	(ii)	(i)
(d)	(iii)	(ii)	(i)	(iv)

105. Job analysis is carried out by:

(a) Organization of tasks
(b) Identification on skills required

Answer

102. (a) 103. (b) 104. (c)

(c) Collection of information related to nature of job
(d) Breaking down of job into parts and further evaluation

106. Effective Management recognizes the validity of:
(a) Values and Standards (b) Management Process
(c) Decision-making (d) Resources

107. Arrange the following teaching learning methods in order of learner's ability:
(i) A video show (ii) Laboratory method
(iii) Demonstration (iv) Radio talk

Codes:
(a) (ii), (i), (iii), (iv) (b) (iv), (i), (iii), (ii)
(c) (ii), (i), (iii), (iv) (d) (ii), (iii), (i), (iv)

108. Decision-making is a process involving following steps in sequence:
(i) Evaluate the alternatives
(ii) Identify the alternatives
(iii) Identify the problem
(iv) Make a decision
(v) Evaluate the decision

Codes:
(a) (ii), (i), (iii), (iv), (v)
(b) (iv), (i), (iii), (ii), (v)
(c) (i), (ii), (iii), (iv), (v)
(d) (iii), (iv), (ii), (i), (v)

109. Steps of curriculum planning are given below. Write them in correct order:
(i) Environment for learning
(ii) Problems/needs of the learner
(iii) Sequencing of contents
(iv) Philosophical frame

Answer

105. (b) 106. (c) 108. (b) 108. (d)

Codes:

(a) (ii), (i), (iv), (iii) (b) (iv), (i), (iii), (ii)
(c) (i), (ii), (iii), (iv) (d) (ii), (iii), (i), (iv)

110. Match the following item in List I with List II:

List I	List II
A. Acting skits	(i) Books and reading material
B. Discussion	(ii) Experience and activities through examination
C. Evaluation	(iii) Individual activity
D. Resources	(iv) Group activity

Codes:	A	B	C	D
(a)	(i)	(iv)	(iii)	(ii)
(b)	(iii)	(iv)	(ii)	(i)
(c)	(iv)	(i)	(iii)	(ii)
(d)	(iii)	(i)	(ii)	(iv)

111. Match the following item:

List I

A. Readymade and homemade
B. Direct experience
C. Dramatized experience
D. Visual symbols

List II

(i) Role of a host (ii) diagrams
(iii) Exhibits (iv) Preparing a meal

Codes:	A	B	C	D
(a)	(i)	(iv)	(iii)	(ii)
(b)	(ii)	(i)	(iv)	(iii)
(c)	(iv)	(i)	(iii)	(ii)
(d)	(iii)	(i)	(ii)	(iv)

Answer

109. (a) 110. (b) 111. (a)

112. Decision-making is based on:
   (a) Relying on popular opinion
   (b) Planning out a path of action
   (c) Choosing among alternative rationally
   (d) None of the above

113. Match the following:

   List I

   A. Innovators B. Laggards
   C. Distance education D. Individual method

   List II

   (i) Last to adopt innovation
   (ii) Adopt new idea
   (iii) Dealing with people individually
   (iv) Educating dispersed people

Codes:	**A**	**B**	**C**	**D**
(a)	(i)	(iv)	(iii)	(ii)
(b)	(ii)	(i)	(iv)	(iii)
(c)	(iv)	(ii)	(i)	(iii)
(d)	(iii)	(i)	(ii)	(iv)

114. Give the correct sequence in employment process:
   (i) Personal records verification
   (ii) Application form
   (iii) Test
   (iv) Advertisement
   (v) Interview

   Codes:

(a)	(i)	(iv)	(iii)	(ii)	(v)
(b)	(iv)	(ii)	(v)	(iii)	(i)
(c)	(iv)	(i)	(iii)	(ii)	(v)
(d)	(iv)	(i)	(ii)	(iv)	(iii)

Answer

112. (c) 113. (c) 114. (b)

115. Write the correct sequence of decision-making process:

(i) Defining the problem
(ii) Selecting an alternative
(iii) Seeking alternative solution
(iv) Accepting responsibility for decision
(v) Thinking through alternatives

(a)	(i)	(iii)	(v)	(ii)	(iv)
(b)	(ii)	(i)	(iv)	(iii)	(v)
(c)	(iv)	(i)	(ii)	(iii)	(v)
(d)	(iii)	(i)	(ii)	(iv)	(v)

116. The most sophisticated style and extremely formal service is:

(a) Waiter service (b) Self-service
(c) Room service (d) Banquet service

117. Long-term and short-term goals are based on:

(a) Continuity (b) Duration
(c) Interdependence (d) All of the above

118. The motivating factors to make decisions and choices are:

(i) Resources (ii) Values
(iii) Goals (iv) Standards

Codes:

(a) (i), (ii) and (iv) are correct
(b) (i), (ii), and (iii) are correct
(c) (ii), (iii) and (iv) are correct
(d) (i), (iii) and (iv) are correct

119. **Assertion (A):** Work simplification is the simplest, easiest and quickest method of doing a task.

Reason (R): Work simplification is a technique for accomplishing a task with least amount of energy.

Answer

115. (a) 116. (d) 117. (c) 118. (b)

(a) (A) is true but (R) is false
(b) (A) is false but (R) is true
(c) Both (A) and (R) are true
(d) Both (A) and (R) are false

120. **Assertion (A):** Pretesting at the beginning of an experiment can produce a change in subjects.

Reason (R): Pretesting may produce a practice effect making subjects more proficient in subsequent test performance.

(a) (A) is true but (R) is false
(b) (A) is false but (R) is true
(c) Both (A) and (R) are false
(d) Both (A) and (R) are true

121. Arrange the correct order of catering personnel according to seniority

(a) Manager, utility worker, cook, supervisor
(b) Manager, cook, supervisor, utility worker
(c) Manager, supervisor, cook, utility worker
(d) Manager, utility worker, supervisor, cook

122. Match the following:

List I	**List II**
A. Horizontal lines	(i) Activity and dignity
B. Vertical lines	(ii) Grace and Flexibility
C. Diagonal lines	(iii) Rest and Repose
D. Curved lines	(iv) Movement and force

Codes:	A	B	C	D
(a)	(iii)	(iv)	(i)	(ii)
(b)	(ii)	(i)	(iv)	(iii)
(c)	(ii)	(i)	(iii)	(iv)
(d)	(iii)	(i)	(ii)	(iv)

Answer

119. (c) 120. (d) 121. (a) 122. (c)

123. One direction that is not ideal for construction of the front of the house is:

(a) North (b) South
(c) East (d) West

124. The level of harmony of feeling is lowest in:

(a) Compromise (b) Dominance
(c) Voluntary submission (d) Integration

125. Match the following:

List I	List II
A. Material Management	(i) Job specification
B. Personnel Management	(ii) Cash book
C. Financial Management	(iii) Production schedule
D. Plant Management	(iv) Insulation
E. Market Management	(v) Discount

Codes:	A	B	C	D	E
(a)	(iii)	(iv)	(i)	(ii)	(v)
(b)	(ii)	(i)	(iv)	(iii)	(v)
(c)	(iii)	(i)	(ii)	(iv)	(v)
(d)	(iii)	(i)	(ii)	(v)	(iv)

126. Match List I with List II:

List I	List II
A. Socialisation	(i) Rules are socially agreed principles
B. Heteronomous Morality	(ii) Unconsciously taking on the style and personality of another person
C. Animism	(iii) Learning social rules and norms
D. Identification	(iv) Belief that non-living objects are living

Codes:	A	B	C	D
(a)	(iii)	(i)	(ii)	(iv)
(b)	(ii)	(i)	(iv)	(iii)

Answer

123. (b) 124. (d) 125. (c)

(c)	(iv)	(i)	(iii)	(ii)
(d)	(iii)	(i)	(ii)	(iv)

127. Match the following:

List I		List II
A. Purpose	(i)	Transferring knowledge
B. Dissemination	(ii)	Logic behind the establishment
C. Execution	(iii)	Knowing the problem
D. Identification	(iv)	Implementation of programme

Codes:	A	B	C	D
(a)	(iii)	(iv)	(i)	(ii)
(b)	(ii)	(i)	(iv)	(iii)
(c)	(ii)	(iv)	(iii)	(i)
(d)	(iii)	(i)	(ii)	(iv)

128. Match the following:

List I		List II
A. $-\chi^2$	(i)	Correlation coefficient
B. r	(ii)	Probability
C. Σ	(iii)	Chi-square
D. P	(iv)	Mean
	(v)	Sum of

Codes:	A	B	C	D
(a)	(iii)	(iv)	(i)	(ii)
(b)	(ii)	(i)	(iv)	(iii)
(c)	(iv)	(i)	(v)	(ii)
(d)	(iii)	(i)	(ii)	(iv)

129. Give the correct sequence involved in work improvement:
(i) Break down the job
(ii) Analyse the job
(iii) Apply the new method
(iv) Work out the method
(v) Select the job

Answer

126. (a) 127. (c) 128. (a)

Codes:

(a) (iv), (i), (ii), (iii), (v)
(b) (v), (i), (ii), (iv), (iii)
(c) (iii), (ii), (i), (iv), (v)
(d) (iii), (iv), (ii), (i), (v)

130. Steps of curriculum planning are given below, write them in correct order:
   (i) Environment for learning
   (ii) Problems/needs of the learner
   (iii) Contents are sequencing of contents
   (iv) Philosophical frame (ideological base)

Codes:

(a) (iv), (i), (ii), (iii) (b) (iv), (iii), (ii), (i)
(c) (iii), (ii), (i), (iv) (d) (iii), (iv), (ii), (i)

131. **Assertion (A):** A process chart is a simple technique for recording and analysing a job.

Reason (R): It uses illustration to describe the process so that the job can be condensed into a compact form.

(a) (A) is true but (R) is false
(b) (A) is false but (R) is true
(c) Both (A) and (R) are true
(d) Both (A) and (R) are false

132. **Assertion (A):** Proper work posture reduces energy requirement.

Reason (R): Proper posture means keeping parts in alignment, therefore reduces energy cost.

(a) (A) is true but (R) is false
(b) (A) is false but (R) is true
(c) Both (A) and (R) are true
(d) Both (A) and (R) are false

Answer

129. (b) 130. (a) 131. (c) 132. (c)

133. **Assertion (A):** Result Demonstration is a method of motivating the people for adoption of a new practice by showing its distinctly superior result.

Reason (R): In result demonstration, actual results are shown, therefore chances of adoption of new practices are more.

(a) (A) is true but (R) is false
(b) (A) is false but (R) is true
(c) Both (A) and (R) are false
(d) Both (A) and (R) are true

134. **Assertion (A):** A campaign is an intense educational activity for motivating and mobilizing a community to action, to solve a problem or satisfy a need urgently felt by it.

Reason (R): A campaign is done to induce emotional participation of the community to create a favourable psychological climate for adoption of new practices.

(a) (A) is true but (R) is false
(b) (A) is false but (R) is true
(c) Both (A) and (R) are true
(d) Both (A) and (R) are false

135. 'Pricing method' of pricing includes—

(a) attempt to add profit to food cost
(b) considers actual labour cost
(c) method used for labour intensive products
(d) adds profits to individual item price

136. **Assertion (A):** A prospects is a formal summary of proposed work.

Reason (R): It is an evaluation tool used by professional for assessment.

(a) (A) is true but (R) is false
(b) (A) is false but (R) is true

Answer

133. (d) 134. (c) 135. (a)

(c) Both (A) and (R) are true
(d) Both (A) and (R) are false

137. Arrange the Employment process in the right sequence:
(i) Induction (ii) Application forms
(iii) Other tests (iv) Interview
(v) Contract negotiations

Codes:

(a) (iv), (i), (ii), (iii), (v) (b) (iv), (iii), (ii), (i), (v)
(c) (iii), (ii), (i), (iv), (v) (d) (ii), (i), (iii), (iv), (v)

138. Arrange different methods of resolving conflict according to the level of satisfaction (less to more):
(i) Compromise (ii) Dominance
(iii) Integration (iv) Voluntary submission
(a) (iv), (i), (ii), (iii) (b) (ii), (iv), (i), (iii)
(c) (iii), (ii), (i), (iv) (d) (iii), (iv), (ii), (i)

139. Match List I with List II:

List I

A. Economic decision B. Individual decision
C. Habitual decision D. Group decision

List II

(i) Automatic type
(ii) Not good as may lead to conflicting situation
(iii) Allocation and exchange of resource use
(iv) Easy to make
(v) Good quality but conflict may occur

Codes:	**A**	**B**	**C**	**D**
(a)	(iii)	(v)	(i)	(ii)
(b)	(ii)	(i)	(iv)	(iii)
(c)	(iii)	(iv)	(i)	(v)
(d)	(iii)	(i)	(v)	(iv)

Answer

136. (a) 137. (d) 138. (b) 139. (c)

140. Match the following:

List I

A. Wechsler scale
B. The perspective of the social group is considered
C. Think of one aspect of a relationship at a time
D. Defects which are results of alcohol consumption

List II

(i) Intelligence
(ii) Centring
(iii) Social conventional role thinking
(iv) Fetal alcohol syndrome (FAS) during pregnancy

Codes:	**A**	**B**	**C**	**D**
(a)	(iii)	(iv)	(i)	(ii)
(b)	(ii)	(i)	(iv)	(iii)
(c)	(ii)	(iii)	(i)	(iv)
(d)	(iii)	(i)	(ii)	(iv)

141. Which of the following is not a management approach:

(a) Classic
(b) System Approach
(c) Human Relation
(d) Double Entry System

142. ABC of Poster:

(a) Attractive, Brief, Clear
(b) Attention, Brief, Clarity
(c) Attractive, Bold, Clear
(d) Attractive, Bold, Colourful

143. Components of implementing are:

(i) Adjusting
(ii) Facilitating
(iii) Controlling
(iv) Checking

Codes:

(a) (i) and (iii) are correct
(b) (ii) and (iii) are correct

Answer

140. (c) 141. (d) 142. (a)

(c) (ii) and (iv) are correct
(d) (iii) and (iv) are correct

144. Aspects of a Good Lesson Plan

(i) Objectives
(ii) Teacher's activities
(iii) Leaning experience
(iv) Teaching aids
(v) Appraisal

Codes:

(a) (i), (iii), (iv) and (v) are correct
(b) (ii), (iii), (iv) and (v) are correct
(c) (i), (iv) and (v) are correct
(d) All of the above

145. Which among the following are the community services offered in the interest of the public:

(i) Protection
(ii) Transport
(iii) Social
(iv) Communication

Codes:

(a) (i) and (iii) are correct
(b) (i), (ii) and (iv) are correct
(c) (i), (ii) and (iii) are correct
(d) (iii), (ii) and (iv) are correct

146. **Assertion (A):** Invoice is a document that comes with supplies.

Reason (R): Cash payment has to be made on the basis of it.

(a) (A) is true but (R) is false
(b) (A) is false but (R) is true
(c) Both (A) and (R) are true
(d) Both (A) and (R) are false

147. **Assertion (A):** Self-concept is an image of a person. It is the way one perceives oneself, one's abilities and limitations.

Answer

143. (b) 144. (d) 145. (b) 146. (a)

Reason (R): Self-concept is the understanding of the self, in comparison to the past self, without social comparison.

(a) (A) is true but (R) is false
(b) (A) is false but (R) is true
(c) Both (A) and (R) are true
(d) Both (A) and (R) are false

148. **Assertion (A):** Electronic media is a mass media.

Reason (R): All mass media are not electronic media.

(a) (A) is true but (R) is false
(b) (A) is false but (R) is true
(c) Both (A) and (R) are true
(d) Both (A) and (R) are false

149. Give the correct sequence of managerial functions listed below:

(i) Reporting (ii) Staffing
(iii) Planning (iv) Organizing
(v) Co-ordinating (vi) Budgeting
(vii) Directing

Codes:

(a) (iii), (iv), (ii), (vii), (v), (i), (vi)
(b) (ii), (i), (iv), (iii), (v), (vi), (vii)
(c) (iii), (iv), (i), (ii), (vii), (v), (vi)
(d) (i), (vii), (ii), (iv), (v), (vi), (iii)

150. Panchayati Raj Institution in the hierarchy of governance from grassroots upwards is:

(i) Gram Sabha (ii) Block Panchayat
(iii) District Panchayat (iv) Gram Panchayat

Codes:

(a) (i), (ii), (iii), (iv) (b) (ii), (i), (iv), (iii)
(c) (i), (iv), (ii), (iii) (d) (i), (iii), (ii), (iv)

151. Match the records List I with the department in List II where they are used:

Answer

147. (a) 148. (c) 149. (a) 150. (c)

List I (Records)	List II (Department)
A. Stock book	(i) Purchase
B. KOT	(ii) Personnel
C. Payroll record	(iii) Store
D. Specifications	(iv) Dining room

Codes:	A	B	C	D
(a)	(iii)	(iv)	(i)	(ii)
(b)	(ii)	(i)	(iv)	(iii)
(c)	(iv)	(i)	(iii)	(ii)
(d)	(iii)	(iv)	(ii)	(i)

152. Conversation is a—
   (a) Listening skill (b) Intellectual skill
   (c) Expressive skill (d) Receptive skill

153. Indicate the region, separating one system from another, in the systems approaches to management:
   (a) Boundary (b) Interface
   (c) Exchanger (d) Divider

154. The process of assessing the progress of a project based on predetermined indicators and objectives of the programme is known as:
   (a) Planning (b) Implementation
   (c) Monitoring (d) Evaluation

155. Performance appraisals and review committees in an organization are example of:
   (a) Outline evaluation (b) Internal evaluation
   (c) External evaluation (d) Summative evaluation

156. Organization chart is also known as:
   (a) Tree chart (b) Flow chart
   (c) Flip chart (d) Striptease chart

Answer

151. (d) 152. (c) 153. (a) 154. (c) 155. (b)
156. (b)

157. Which of the following are not used for financial management?

(i) Variable cost (ii) Trial balance
(iii) Performance appraisal (iv) Fixed cost
(v) Break-even analysis (vi) SWOT

Codes:

(a) (i) and (vi) (b) (iii) and (vi)
(c) (i), (ii) and (vi) (d) (v), (vi) and (ii)

158. Dominant emotions are always:

(i) Pleasant (ii) Unpleasant
(iii) Strong (iv) Rare

Codes:

(a) (ii), (iii) and (iv) are correct
(b) (i), (ii) and (iii) are correct
(c) (ii) and (iv) are correct
(d) All are correct

159. The affective components of workers are:

(i) Attitudes (ii) Skills
(iii) Feelings (iv) Interests

Codes:

(a) (i), (iii) and (iv) are correct
(b) (i), (ii) and (iv) correct
(c) (i), (ii) and (iii) are correct
(d) (ii) and (iv) are correct

160. Goals of the elderly include:

(i) Family relations (ii) Good health
(iii) Education (iv) Vocational pursuits

Codes:

(a) (i) and (iii) (b) (i) and (ii)
(c) (ii) and (iii) (d) (iv)

Answer

157. (b) 158. (b) 159. (a) 160. (b)

161. Voluntary organizations are involved in the following activities:

(i) Welfare
(ii) Policy decision-making
(iii) Advocacy
(iv) Networking

Codes:

(a) (i), (ii) and (iii)
(b) (ii), (iv) and (iii)
(c) (iii), (i) and (ii)
(d) (i), (iii) and (iv)

162. **Assertion (A):** Ergonomics is also referred to as 'Human Factors'.

Reason (R): The focus of the study is on worker fatigue.

(a) (A) is true but (R) is wrong
(b) (A) is false but (R) is true
(c) Both (A) and (R) are true
(d) Both (A) and (R) are wrong

163. **Assertion (A):** Need assessment is carried out to identify the gap between the present and the desired situation.

Reason (R): Objectives of programme planning are based on need assessment.

(a) (A) is true but (R) is false
(b) (A) is false but (R) is true
(c) Both (A) and (R) are true
(d) Both (A) and (R) are false

164. Arrange in the right sequence the steps taken in planning a physical facility for food service unit:

(i) Planning team
(ii) Manu Analysis
(iii) Architectural Features
(iv) Prospectus
(v) Budget
(vi) Feasibility study

Codes:

(a) (i), (ii), (iii), (iv), (v), (vi)
(b) (iv), (i), (vi), (ii), (iii), (v)
(c) (iii), (iv), (i), (ii), (vi), (v)
(d) (i), (iii), (ii), (iv), (v), (vi)

Answer

161. (d) 162. (a) 163. (c) 164. (b)

165. The storeroom inventory is recorded in:
    (a) Journal (b) Cash book
    (c) Ledger (d) Bincards

166. Contingency approach of Management holds:
    (a) that job should be segmented
    (b) that organization should be seen as whole
    (c) that activities to be adjusted to suit situations
    (d) that productivity is increased by opportunity

167. Doing many activities together is called:
    (a) Grouping (b) Combining
    (c) Dovetailing (d) All the above

168. Triggering the mind of participants to finding out solutions for a problem is called as:
    (a) Brain storming (b) Debate
    (c) Symposium (d) Colloquism

169. The record of food store inventory is kept in:
    (a) Ledger (b) Stock register
    (c) Cash Book (d) Journal

170. The scientific study of man and his working environment is:
    (a) Demography (b) Work simplication
    (c) Ergonomics (d) Occupational health

171. The component of controlling in which actions and outputs are examined in compliance with standard is:
    (a) Adjusting (b) Changing
    (c) Checking (d) Assessing

172. Eliminating or combining parts of jobs is suggested by incorporating changes in:
    (a) Tools (b) Posture
    (c) Production sequence (d) Raw materials

Answer

165. (c) 166. (d) 167. (a) 168. (d) 169. (b)
170. (c) 171. (a) 172. (c)

173. **Assertion (A):** The success of an extension programme depends on the involvement on the leader in the programme.

Reason (R): An active mass following and participation makes any programme success.

(a) (A) is true but (R) is false
(b) (A) is false but (R) is true
(c) Both (A) and (R) are false
(d) Both (A) and (R) are true

174. **Assertion (A):** The quality of decision determine the quality of management.

Reason (R): Decision-making occurs when there is a problem to solve or some choice to make.

(a) (A) is true but (R) is false
(b) (A) is false but (R) is true
(c) Both (A) and (R) are true
(d) Both (A) and (R) are false

175. The tool of Management that does not deal with personnel:

(i) Organization chart (ii) Production schedule
(iii) Job description (iv) Job specification
(v) Budget (vi) Communication

Codes:

(a) (i) and (iii) (b) (iv), (vi) and (iii)
(c) (iii), (iv) and (ii) (d) (ii) and (v)

176. **Assertion (A):** All individuals in a social system do not adopt an innovation at the same time.

Reason (R): But they adopt innovation in an ordered time sequence.

(a) (A) is true but (R) is false
(b) (A) is false but (R) is true
(c) Both (A) and (R) are true
(d) Both (A) and (R) are false

Answer

173. (d) 174. (a) 175. (d) 176. (c)

177. Arrange the stages of the adoption process in correct sequence:

(i) Interest (ii) Awareness
(iii) Evaluation (iv) Adoption
(v) Trial

Codes:

(a) (ii), (i), (iii), (v), (iv)
(b) (iv), (iii), (ii), (i), (v)
(c) (iii), (ii), (i), (v), (iv)
(d) (iii), (iv), (ii), (i), (v)

178. Sequence the scales of measurement from the lowest to the highest:

(i) Interval scale (ii) Ordinal scale
(iii) Nominal scale (iv) Ratio scale

Codes:

(a) (iv), (i), (ii), (iii) (b) (iv), (iii), (ii), (i)
(c) (iii), (ii), (i), (iv) (d) (iii), (iv), (ii), (i)

179. Match the List I with List II:

List I	**List II**
A. Change in knowledge	(i) Self-reliance
B. Change in attitude	(ii) Doing things
C. Change in confidence	(iii) What people know
D. Change in skill	(iv) Reaction towards certain things

Codes:	A	B	C	D
(a)	(ii)	(iv)	(i)	(iii)
(b)	(ii)	(i)	(iv)	(iii)
(c)	(iii)	(iv)	(i)	(ii)
(d)	(iii)	(i)	(ii)	(iv)

Answer

177. (a) 178. (c) 179. (c)

Chapter 6

Resource Management and Human Development

1. Unconscious memories are memories that:
   (a) You can't remember but can make you feel scared
   (b) Are created when the hippocampus and cerebral cortex are not involved
   (c) Are stored in the amygdala and its related parts
   (d) All the above
2. Which of the following is controlled by the cerebral cortex?
   (a) Movement
   (b) Memory
   (c) Emotions
   (d) Intelligence
3. How can health improvements be quantified and measured?
   (a) We cannot
   (b) Using quality and length of life
   (c) Comparing health status to the state of complete physical, mental and social well-being
   (d) Using only monetary terms
4. If a baby has very frightening things happen to it often enough it can cause
   (a) Certain brain pathways to develop
   (b) Certain brain pathways not to develop
   (c) Permanent changes in the brain
   (d) All the above

Answer

1. (a) 2. (a) 3. (c) 4. (d)

5. The contra indications to cardiovascular machines include:
   (a) Wearing incorrect trainers
   (b) Cardiovascular problems
   (c) Bending too far over on the rowing machine
   (d) Incorrect height on the bike
6. To prevent the spread of HIV infection it is vital to:
   (a) Know the ways by which HIV is spread
   (b) Combat the superstitions and taboos related to sexual orientation
   (c) Contradict the persisting myths about HIV and AIDS
   (d) All of the above
7. Encouraging or enforcing independence in our babies and young children promotes:
   (a) Emotional maturity
   (b) Independence
   (c) Instills a fundamental belief that their needs will not be met
   (d) All of the above
8. As men age, they tend to accumulate more fat in the:
   (a) Hips and thighs (b) Waist
   (c) Calves (d) None of the above
9. Duty of care means:
   (a) Accepting responsibility for other people's mistakes
   (b) Giving out advice and relevant accident forms to injured members
   (c) Having a working knowledge of rules
   (d) Accepting responsibility for health and safety in workplace
10. What symptom of Alzheimer's is present from beginning to end?
   (a) Argumentativeness (b) Poor hygiene
   (c) Wandering (d) Loss of interest and initiative

Answer

5. (b) 6. (d) 7. (d) (8) (b) 9. (d)
10. (d)

11. What is the best way to prevent back injury?
    (a) Exercise to strengthen your back and reduce stress
    (b) Lose excess weight
    (c) Maintain good posture
    (d) All of the above

12. In addition to diabetes, health problems associated with obesity in children include:
    (a) Increased infections, anaemia and blood clots
    (b) Hardening of the arteries, early puberty and abnormal skeletal development
    (c) Vertigo, nausea and amblyopia
    (d) Chronic hiccups

13. What percentage of our daily calorie intake (energy) should come from carbohydrates?
    (a) 50 per cent (b) 80 per cent
    (c) 100 per cent (d) Zero per cent

14. Dentists recommend that you brush your teeth
    (a) Twice a day
    (b) After each and every meal
    (c) When you start getting a funny taste in your mouth
    (d) It's a personal preference and varies among people

15. Which of the following puts your heart at risk?
    (a) Cigarette smoking (b) High blood pressure
    (c) High cholesterol levels (d) All of the above

16. Some babies who are just beginning to develop emotional attachments and some degree of communication have a difficult time with strangers. Why is this?
    (a) The stranger may not hold the baby properly
    (b) The stranger may miss subtle cues from the baby and then not meet the baby's expectations. This may confuse the baby

Answer

11. (d) 12. (b) 13. (a) 14. (b) 15. (d)

(c) The stranger may look like someone the baby does not like
(d) The stranger's voice may be upsetting to the baby

17. How has evolution determined a baby's needs?
(a) Evolution has nothing to do with the needs of today's babies
(b) Continental drift
(c) Only the babies that survived had children
(d) Global warming

18. The younger sibling learns eventually that he or she too can be aggressive rind cause problems for the older sibling. At what age does this usually occur?
(a) 10 to 12 months (b) 12 to 14 months
(c) 14 to 16 months (d) Over 16 months

19. The younger sibling eventually learns to get the parents help when being bothered by the older sibling. At which stage does this occur?
(a) Between 11 and 13 months
(b) Before 10 months of age
(c) Between 16 and 18 months
(d) None of the above

20. Breast feeding is often blamed for:
(a) Lack of sleep
(b) Headaches
(c) Marriage problems
(d) All the above

21. Developing the capacity for attachment in the earliest years of life is important because:
(a) It is the only time a person can develop the capacity to have intimate, loving relationships
(b) Intimate attachments with other human beings are the most fundamental source of satisfaction in life

Answer

16. (b) 17. (c) 18. (d) 19. (c) 20. (d)

(c) Human beings have evolved as social animals and anything that interferes with their capacity to be social runs against human nature
(d) All the above

22. Isotonic exercise is an exercise where
(a) A muscle changes in length but the tone remains the same
(b) The length of the muscle does not change but there is a change in the tone
(c) The tone of the muscle is constant
(d) The muscle becomes longer and thicker as the origin and insertion move away from each other

23. What a baby experiences in infancy can
(a) Affect its IQ
(b) Determine which brain pathways develop
(c) Affect its capacity to form loving relationships as an adult
(d) All of the above

24. Bipolar neurons are nerve cells that have
(a) a single dendrite at the end of the cell and single axon at the other
(b) several axons and a single dendrite
(c) many dendrites and a single neuron
(d) a single branch which after leaving the cell body divides into two directions

25. Developmental change is commonly characterized by
(a) Growth (b) Orderly progression
(c) Differentiation (d) All of the above

26. What is a blood clot?
(a) A blockage in a blood vessel
(b) Blood that has thickened into a soft clump

Answer

21. (d) 22. (b) 23. (c) 24. (d) 25. (d)

(c) An impurity in blood
(d) A scab

27. Which statement is false?
    (a) Vertigo can occur in children as young as 18 months
    (b) Vertigo attacks may last anywhere from a few minutes to several days
    (c) Vertigo can be very uncomfortable, but never life-threatening
    (d) Benign positional vertigo is common among older people

28. What causes vertigo?
    (a) Insufficient rest
    (b) An inner-ear problem
    (c) Poor diet
    (d) Excessive weight

29. Symptoms of a fracture:
    (a) Pain and tenderness
    (b) Possible bleeding at wound site
    (c) Deformity and swelling at wound site
    (d) Possible discoloration

30. Most deaths from heart attacks occur
    (a) In 1-2 hours after attack
    (b) In 15-30 minutes after attack
    (c) Within 24 hours of attack
    (d) Within an hour of attack

31. What is the definition of shock?
    (a) Loss of effective circulation
    (b) Severe injury
    (c) A reaction of a traumatic event
    (d) Severe infection

32. In a secondary assessment you need to look, listen and feel. What are you feeling for?

Answer

26. (b) 27. (a) 28. (b) 29. (c) 30. (d)
31. (a)

(a) Any movement of air from patient's mouth or nose
(b) Deformity, texture, temperature or swelling
(c) Patient's breathe on your cheek
(d) Patient's responses and sounds

33. One of the most important but often neglected aspects of first aid treatment is
(a) Calling for help
(b) Reassuring the patient
(c) Checking for danger
(d) Assessing the patient

34. Why do we dream?
(a) To stimulate our brain during sleep
(b) To fulfill wishes and desires
(c) To maintain our memory function
(d) No one knows for sure

35. What can lead to athlete's foot?
(a) Poor hygiene
(b) Wearing the same pair of shoes every day
(c) Wearing socks made of synthetic fibres
(d) All of the above

36. Isometric exercise is an exercise where
(a) A muscle changes in length but the tone remains the same
(b) The length of the muscle does not change but there is a change in the tone
(c) The tone of the muscle is constant
(d) The muscle becomes longer and thicker as the origin and insertion move away from each other

37. What is it called when the lining of the uterus breaks down and slowly flows from the vagina over a period of three to eight days?

Answer

32. (d) 33. (b) 34. (d) 35. (c) 36. (b)

(a) Ovulation (b) Menstruation
(c) Fertilization (d) None of these

38. What is the relationship between health and health care according to the theory of the "household production of health"?
    (a) Health is related to the house environment
    (b) General living conditions improve health
    (c) There is no relationship
    (d) None of these

39. Which of the following is best to give to breast feeding newborn babies?
    (a) Water (b) Formula
    (c) Sugar water (d) None of these

40. If two-year-olds show resentment toward a younger sibling, what may this indicate?
    (a) It may show that the older child has formed normal, beneficial ties to the parents
    (b) It may show that two-year-olds have not been taught to be tolerant of others
    (c) It may show that the parents display resentment toward some people and the two-year-old has learned this type of behaviour from them
    (d) It may show that two-year-olds like older people, because they can help them, and younger people they feel, are of no value to them

41. Attunement is a term referring to
    (a) A tune that mother, father and baby all like
    (b) A tune that is meant to soothe the baby
    (c) When the signals from mother to baby and baby to mother are properly matched
    (d) When a father has fallen in love with his baby

Answer

37. (b) 38. (b) 39. (b) 40. (a) 41. (c)

42. The peripheral nervous system is divided into 3 further systems. Which of the following is not one of these three systems?
    (a) Cranial nerves
    (b) Spinal nerves
    (c) Precentral nervous system
    (d) Autonomic nervous system
43. You should exercise at least
    (a) Two days/week (b) Three days/week
    (c) Four days/week (d) Five days/week
44. The treatment of a major fracture to a limb includes:
    (a) Immobilizing the injured limb in as natural a position as possible
    (b) A compression bandage layered away from the heart over the site to restrict swelling
    (c) Always splinting to another limb
    (d) Elevation of the limb and giving pain relieving medication
45. After managing life threatening problems the casualty should be examined in which order:
    (a) Head, arms, chest, back, abdomen and legs
    (b) Head, chest, arms, abdomen, legs and back
    (c) Head, chest, abdomen, arms, legs and back
    (d) Head, arms, legs, abdomen, chest and back
46. The treatment for a conscious patient who has suffered chest pains includes:
    (a) Place patient in a comfortable position, leaning forward pinching the nostrils and encourage breathing with short breaths to alleviate pain
    (b) Loosen clothing, place patient on back with head and shoulders slightly raised and a blanket under the knees

Answer

42. (c) 43. (b) 44. (a) 45. (c)

(c) Place patient on side as soon as possible, manage any injuries, monitor ABC and seek medical aid
(d) Place patient in a comfortable position, give oxygen therapy, loosen tight clothing, and reassure the patient

47. Who needs the most calcium?
(a) 14-18-year olds (b) 19-50-year olds
(c) Those 51 and over (d) All of the above

48. Which of the following statements is true?
(a) A breast feeding mother has to be extremely careful about what she eats
(b) Women with small breasts make less milk than those with large breasts
(c) A mother who smokes is better not to breast feed
(d) None of the above

49. Which specific massage movement would be most beneficial to relieve tense quadriceps muscles?
(a) Effleurage (b) Hacking
(c) Kneading (d) Vibrations

50. Babies who sleep alone are often under stress. The biggest problem with that is:
(a) They might grow up to be poor sleepers
(b) Stress produces cortisol, and too much cortisol can damage the brain and cause permanent problems
(c) They might chew the bars of their crib
(d) They might get used to being alone and not want to be with other people

51. Gum disease is caused by:
(a) A buildup of bacteria-laden tartar on teeth and below the gum line
(b) Eating too much candy
(c) Not brushing your teeth
(d) Gingivitis

Answer

46. (c) 47. (a) 48. (a) 49. (c) 50. (d)
51. (a)

52. How much water do experts reckon people should drink every day?
    (a) 1 liter (b) 2 liters
    (c) 3 liters (d) 10 liters
53. Do active people or inactive people have a higher bone density?
    (a) Active (b) Inactive
    (c) Can't say (d) None of these
54. Do larger or smaller women have an increased risk of osteoporosis?
    (a) Larger (b) Smaller
    (c) Can't say (d) None of these
55. You watch a new TV programme with enthusiasm. You then watch a second similar programme. You later find it difficult to remember the details of the second programme in that things about the first keep intruding. What probably has occurred?
    (a) Proactive interference
    (b) Trace consolidation
    (c) Mnemonic transfer
    (d) Decay of memory trace
56. A person infected with HIV
    (a) May live for many years after infection
    (b) Should have symptoms
    (c) Ultimately dies because of AIDS
    (d) (a) and (c)
57. A person infected with HIV
    (a) Can always transmit the infection to others
    (b) Can only transmit the infection at the last stage of the infection (AIDS stage)

Answer

52. (b) 53. (a) 54. (a) 55. (a) 56. (d)

(c) Can only transmit the infection in the first six months after the infection
(d) (a) and (b)

58. What might smelly feel indicate?
(a) Liver problems (b) Allergies
(c) Kidney problems (d) Arthritis

59. Which of the following problems might be the result of an infant failing to develop a sense of trust and emotional security?
(a) Needing a very expensive car
(b) Low self-esteem
(c) An inability to maintain lasting relationships
(d) All the above

60. What is the most important decision for a pregnant woman to make?
(a) What medicine to take for pain
(b) How much weight to gain
(c) Who will be your birth attendant
(d) What vitamins to take

61. What different types of places can you have your baby?
(a) Hospital (b) Home
(c) Birth centre (d) All of these

62. What does it mean that babies in a sling spend more time in the "quiet alert" state?
(a) The baby is in a safe place because the parent is alert
(b) Babies know that they must be quiet and alert or they may get placed in their crib
(c) Babies who are regularly worn are known to be more alert and aware of their surroundings more often
(d) Babies who are worn in slings are smarter

Answer

57. (a) 58. (c) 59. (c) 60. (b) 61. (d)
62. (c)

63. What is the longest length of time that the effects of being too closely spaced might affect siblings?
    (a) A few months (b) About a year
    (c) Several years (d) A lifetime

64. Why do children of hurtful parents sometimes blame themselves for abuse they suffered from their parents?
    (a) Because of original sin
    (b) Because they really did deserve being abused
    (c) Because it is too frightening to believe the parent can't be trusted
    (d) Because children can't stink straight until they are grown-up

65. A supportive and involved father, grandparents, aunts and uncles, neighbors and friends living in a community that values and supports mothering is important.
    (a) Not necessarily (b) Possibly
    (c) Sometimes (d) Always

66. At birth the newborn baby's brain is:
    (a) Fully developed
    (b) As developed as it ever will be
    (c) Not developed at all
    (d) None of the above

67. If the amygdala has been conditioned by fearful experiences it can
    (a) make the hippocampus act like a sea and horse
    (b) make it very difficult or impossible to remove the force of unremembered fears
    (c) require a really good therapist to help the person get over it
    (d) help the person remember the details of the fearful experiences

Answer

63. (d) 64. (c) 65. (d) 66. (a) 67. (b)

68. Because of the way human beings have evolved, which of the following are babies genetically programmed to need?
    (a) Formula (b) Mother's milk
    (c) A crib (d) A room of their own

69. Which of the following types of aggression can be summarized as "aggression intended to harm another person"?
    (a) Instrumental aggression
    (b) Hostile aggression
    (c) Overt aggression
    (d) Relational aggression

70. Which of the following is not one of the phases of attachment development?
    (a) Pre-attachment
    (b) Perceptual selecting
    (c) Attachment in the making
    (d) Goal-corrected partnership

71. Children begin to display the evidence of a true separation attachment bond through separation anxiety at around
    (a) birth (b) 4-6 months
    (c) 6-8 months (d) 8-10 months

72. Which of these terms represent the moral branch of our functioning?
    (a) Id (b) Superego
    (c) Ego (d) Alter ego

73. Which of the following is an obsession?
    (a) Persistent doubts about whether the stove was turned off that morning
    (b) Persistent checking for one of the keys
    (c) Persistent hand washing
    (d) Persistent singing

Answer

68. (b) 69. (b) 70. (d) 71. (d) 72. (a)
73. (c)

74. Men and women show equal levels of aggression:
    (a) When they are provoked
    (b) When they believe they are not being observed
    (c) When the form of aggression is indirect
    (d) When they display emotional aggression
75. Non-verbal cues are most likely to indicators of:
    (a) Traits (b) Needs
    (c) Temporary moods (d) Gait
76. The major cause of high blood pressure is:
    (a) A kidney abnormality
    (b) An enlarged heart
    (c) A defect in the aorta
    (d) Unknown
77. A common symptom of high blood pressure is:
    (a) Headache (b) Dizziness
    (c) Rapid heartbeat (d) All of the above
78. High blood pressure:
    (a) Increases the heart's workload
    (b) Causes the heart to enlarge and weaken over time
    (c) Increases the risk of stroke, heart attack, kidney failure and congestive heart failure
    (d) All the above
79. Most cholesterol is produced by
    (a) Kidneys (b) Spleen
    (c) Liver (d) Pancreas
80. High blood cholesterol is a risk factor for
    (a) Atherosclerosis (clogged arteries)
    (b) Stroke
    (c) Heart attack
    (d) All the above

Answer

74. (a) 75. (a) 76. (a) 77. (d) 78. (d)
79. (c) 80. (d)

81. The highest risk factor for stroke is:
   (a) High red blood cell count
   (b) Smoking
   (c) High blood pressure
   (d) Heart disease

82. How many servings of the bread/cereal group should you eat each day?
   (a) 1-3 (b) 4-8
   (c) 6-11 (d) 12-15

83. The earliest signs of skin cancer are:
   (a) The development of actinic keratoses
   (b) The development of a purple rash
   (c) A bad sunburn
   (d) All of the above

84. Which of the following factors is considered a risk factor for cervical cancer?
   (a) Having sex at an early age
   (b) Having multiple sexual partners
   (c) Smoking cigarettes
   (d) All of the above

85. Which of the following affects your risk of osteoporosis?
   (a) Calcium intake (b) Smoking
   (c) Eating disorder (d) All of the above

86. Which one of the following can be a factor in causing bad breath?
   (a) Dry mouth (b) Dieting
   (c) Hormone fluctuations (d) All of the above

87. When a man gains weight, he tends to accumulate fat
   (a) In the hips and buttocks
   (b) Around the waist

Answer

81. (c) 82. (b) 83. (b) 84. (d) 85. (d)
86. (d)

(c) In the arms, legs and face
(d) All of the above

88. Is a hot or warm shower better for dry skin?
(a) Hot
(b) Warm
(c) Both (a) and (b)
(d) None of these

89. What are the two best ways to prevent osteoporosis without hormone replacement?
(a) Calcium or calcium supplements and weight-bearing exercise
(b) Protein and aerobic exercise
(c) Both of these
(d) None of these

90. How many moles does the average person have?
(a) 10 to 15
(b) 20 to 40
(c) 50 to 100
(d) A number roughly equivalent to their age

91. Which statement is false?
(a) Arthritis affects more men than women
(b) Most cases of arthritis are not preventable
(c) An overweight person has a greater chance of developing arthritis than someone of normal weight
(d) Rheumatoid arthritis is the most disabling form of arthritis

92. How can you get rid of a mole?
(a) Rub it with Australian tea tree oil
(b) Cover it with duct tape for a month or so
(c) Have it surgically removed by a physician
(d) Spray a little Windex on it

Answer

87. (b) 88. (b) 89. (a) 90. (b) 91. (a)
92. (c)

93. When people quit using drugs:
    (a) They return to normal
    (b) Their problems with addiction are over
    (c) Their disease is in remission
    (d) Their brain is in mess
94. Which group is most at risk of developing an eating disorder?
    (a) Highly aggressive adolescent girls
    (b) Shy, passive teen girls
    (c) Homosexual teen girls
    (d) Preteen girls from low-income families
95. What percentage of our body fat and shape (apple or pear) is attributable to genes?
    (a) 10 to 15 per cent (b) 20 to 25 per cent
    (c) 50 to 75 per cent (d) 100 per cent
96. How much cooked, skinless poultry, seafood or lean meat should you eat per serving?
    (a) 8 ounces (b) 2 to 3 ounces
    (c) 10 to 12 ounces (d) 4 to 6 ounces
97. What is arthritis?
    (a) Muscle inflammation
    (b) Enlarged bones
    (c) Joint inflammation
    (d) Arthur's disease
98. Which sentence is true?
    (a) Dietary guidelines recommend five to nine servings of fruits and vegetables daily
    (b) Dietary guidelines recommend three to five servings of fruits and vegetables daily
    (c) One cup of blueberries equals one serving of fruit
    (d) A potato does not count as a vegetable serving

Answer

93. (c) 94. (a) 95. (b) 96. (b) 97. (c)
98. (b)

99. Symptoms of shock include:
    (a) rapid, weak pulse
    (b) confusion
    (c) pale, cold clammy skin
    (d) breathless and nausea

100. What is the definition of shock?
    (a) Loss of effective circulation
    (b) Severe injury
    (c) A reaction of a traumatic event
    (d) Severe infection

101. In a secondary assessment you need to look, listen and feel. What are you feeling for?
    (a) Any movement of air from patient's mouth or nose
    (b) Deformity, texture, temperature or swelling
    (c) Patient's breathe on your cheek
    (d) Patient's responses and sounds

102. The treatment of a sprain
    (a) Immobilize
    (b) Stretch the muscle
    (c) Apply ice, elevation and compression
    (d) Apply heat, elevation and compression

103. What is the most correct procedure for first aid documentation?
    (a) Gather information from bystanders and record in patrol log book
    (b) Record events as witnessed, signed by first aider and kept on file
    (c) Check with patient as to cause of injury, ensure next of kin notified and verbally pass information onto ambulance/paramedics
    (d) Record all events as stated by bystanders and ensure patient signs as correct record

Answer

99. (c) 100. (a) 101. (d) 102. (c) 103. (b)

104. Developmental change is commonly characterized by
   (a) Growth (b) Orderly progression
   (c) Differentiation (d) All of the above

105. Which of the following household equipment is a time and energy saving device?
   (a) Pressure cooker (b) Telephone
   (c) DVD Player (d) TV

106. What happens in dextrinization?
   (a) Coagulation (b) Gel formation
   (c) Denaturation (d) None of these

107. Which blood vessel in human body would normally carry the largest amount of urea?
   (a) Dorsal Aorta (b) Hepatic Vein
   (c) Renal Vein (d) Hepatic Portal Vein

108. Total protein synthesised during pregnancy is:
   (a) 900 gm (b) 700 gm
   (c) 1200 gm (d) 1500 gm

109. The kidney, threshold value for sugar is:
   (a) 110-140 mlg/dl (b) 160-170 mlg/dl
   (c) 100-150 mlg/dl (d) 200-250 mlg/dl

110. The basic food items are like "Atta, Suji, Milk, Edible oils" are standardized and marketed under the marks:
   (a) AGMARK (b) ISI
   (c) FPO (d) BIS

111. Teething in babies start at the age of:
   (a) 1 month (b) 3 months
   (c) 6 months (d) 10 months

112. For the development of a child, following are important:
   (a) Parents (b) School
   (c) Society (d) All of the above

Answer

104. (d) 105. (a) 106. (c) 107. (c) 108. (b)
109. (b) 110. (a) 111. (c) 112. (d)

113. Sugar disease is called:
   (a) Jaundice (b) Diabetes
   (c) Typhoid (d) Hysteria

114. Growth refers to:
   (a) Quantitative change
   (b) Directional change
   (c) Longitudinal change
   (d) Qualitative change

115. Community development programme started on:
   (a) 2nd October, 1950
   (b) 25th March, 1950
   (c) 2nd October, 1952
   (d) 2nd October, 1964

116. Red colour matter in fruits and vegetables is due to presence of .... pigments.
   (a) Flavin and Flavinoids (b) Chlorophyll
   (c) Anthocyanins (d) All the above

117. Blood vessels which bring blood to the heart are:
   (a) Arteries (b) Veins
   (c) Capillaries (d) Nerves

118. In modern times there is increase in:
   (a) Nuclear family (b) Joint family
   (c) Both (a) and (b) (d) None of these

119. The first yellow milk that comes out of breast of mother is:
   (a) Serum (b) Cholesterol
   (c) Colostrum (d) Sterol

120. Colon cancer occurs more commonly in:
   (a) Men (b) Women
   (c) Both men and women (d) None of these

Answer

113. (b) 114. (a) 115. (c) 116. (c) 117. (b)
118. (a) 119. (c) 120. (c)

121. Which statement is true?
   (a) The faecal occult blood test is a colon cancer screening method used to detect the presence of abnormal cell development in faeces
   (b) Stools the thickness of pencils are a symptom of colon cancer
   (c) The common treatment for colon cancer is a permanent colostomy, where the entire lower colon is removed and a special bag is worn outside the body to collect waste
   (d) The American Cancer Society recommends that men start regular screening for colon cancer at age 50 and women at age 55

122. What can cause heartburn?
   (a) Eating chocolate
   (b) Eating small, frequent meals
   (c) Going to bed hours after eating
   (d) Wearing loose-fitting clothing

123. The first reported epidemics of dengue fever occurred:
   (a) In the Holy Roman Empire during the 10th century
   (b) In Latin America and South America at the turn of the 19th and 20th centuries
   (c) In Asia, Africa and North America during the late 1700s
   (d) Among English peasants during the reign of King George III

124. What are symptoms of a hernia?
   (a) Heartburn, frequent belching, difficulty in swallowing
   (b) Pain, loss of appetite; dizziness
   (c) Protrusion, headache, diarrhoea
   (d) Frequent urination, extreme thirst, vomiting

Answer

121. (c) 122. (a) 123. (c) 124. (c)

125. How can you prevent calluses and corns from forming?
    (a) Never walk long distances
    (b) Wear socks made of wool or synthetic fibres to keep your feet moist
    (c) Wear shoes that allow your toes to wiggle freely
    (d) All of the above

126. HIV/AIDS is
    (a) One of the greatest challenges facing the world in the 21st century
    (b) An emergency of an unprecedented nature
    (c) A global disaster and threat to the world population
    (d) All of the above

127. Which of these is a good cholesterol fraction?
    (a) Low density lipoprotein cholesterol
    (b) Very low density lipoprotein
    (c) High density lipoprotein
    (d) Triglycerides

128. In Bowlby's view of attachment, the infant's initial behaviour of maintaining proximity to its mother is due to:
    (a) Learning
    (b) Genetics
    (c) Instinct
    (d) Reinforcement

129. **Assertion (A):** Hemispheric specialization begins early in life.

    Reason (R): The left hemisphere of the motor cortex controls the left side of the body and the right side of the body is controlled by right hemisphere since early stage.
    (a) (A) is true but (R) is false
    (b) (A) is false but (R) is true
    (c) Both (A) and (R) are true
    (d) Both (A) and (R) are false

Answer

125. (d) 126. (d) 127. (d) 128. (c) 129. (a)

130. Identify the correct sequence:

The steps in managing the home are:

(i) Planning (ii) Supervision
(iii) Controlling (iv) Evaluation

Codes:

(a) (i), (ii), (iii), (iv) (b) (i), (iii), (ii), (iv)
(c) (ii), (i), (iii), (iv) (d) (ii), (iii), (i), (iv)

131. Indicate the sequence of the steps followed while constructing a house:

(i) Requirements of the family
(ii) Selecting the area/site
(iii) Planning the budget for home
(iv) Selecting the material

Codes:

(a) (i), (iii), (ii), (iv) (b) (i), (ii), (iii), (iv)
(c) (ii), (i), (iii), (iv) (d) (ii), (iii), (i), (iv)

132. Identify the hormone associated with maintaining the blood glucose level in the human body:

(a) Estrogen (b) Glucagon
(c) Calcitonin (d) Parathyroid hormone

133. Rhythm in design cannot be attained by:

(a) Continuous line (b) Contrast
(c) Gradation (d) Repetition

134. According to Erikson, infancy is characterized by development of a sense of:

(a) Self (b) Autonomy
(c) Trust (d) Self-reliance

135. Which of the following tests is used to determine association on the basis of ordinal level of measurement?

(a) Yule's co-efficient
(b) Contingency co-efficient

Answer

130. (b) 131. (a) 132. (b) 133. (b) 134. (c)

(c) Gamma co-efficient
(d) Phi co-efficient

136. **Assertion (A):** Both calcium and vitamin D are required for strong bones and teeth.

Reason (R): Vitamin D helps in absorption of calcium in gut.

(a) (A) is true but (R) is false
(b) (A) is false but (R) is true
(c) Both (A) and (R) are true
(d) Both (A) and (R) are false

137. **Assertion (A):** Fragile X syndrome is more frequent in males than females.

Reason (R): X chromosome is narrowed in some areas and lead to a variety of physical, psychological and social problems.

(a) Both (A) and (R) are true
(b) (A) is true but (R) is false
(c) (A) is false but (R) is true
(d) Both (A) and (R) are false

138. **Assertion (A):** The ego is rational, controlling component of the personality.

Reason (R): Ego operates on the basis of the pleasure principle and control personality.

(a) Both (A) and (R) are true
(b) (A) is true but (R) is false
(c) (A) is false but (R) is true
(d) Both (A) and (R) are false

139. Arrange in sequence the Hierarchy of Health workers:

(i) Anganwadi worker (ii) Supervisor
(iii) CDPO (iv) Multipurpose worker

Answer

135. (d) 136. (c) 137. (a) 138. (b)

Codes:

(a) (i), (iv), (iii), (ii) (b) (i), (iii), (ii), (iv)
(c) (ii), (i), (iii), (iv) (d) (iii), (ii), (iv), (i)

140. Match the name of scientists (List I) with their contribution (List II):

List I

A. Gross & Crandall B. Baluchar Mundelies
C. Lilian Gilbreth D. Longworth & Barrott

List II

(i) Simple pen and pencil technique
(ii) Concept of home management
(iii) Energy cost of household work
(iv) Classes of change

Codes:	**A**	**B**	**C**	**D**
(a)	(ii)	(iv)	(i)	(iii)
(b)	(ii)	(i)	(iv)	(iii)
(c)	(i)	(ii)	(iv)	(iii)
(d)	(iii)	(i)	(ii)	(iv)

141. Mental Retardation is an indicator of deficiency of:

(a) Vitamin A (b) Iodine
(c) Calcium (d) Iron

142. **Assertion (A):** An experienced homemaker works with great care and there is an element of natural rhythm in her normal domestic activities.

Reason (R): In rhythmic work each muscle alternatively gets its chance to rest for an instant.

(a) (A) is true but (R) is false
(b) (A) is false but (R) is true
(c) Both (A) and (R) are true
(d) Both (A) and (R) are false

Answer

139. (d) 140. (a) 141. (b) 142. (d)

143. **Assertion (A):** Adolescent development takes place in social context.

Reason (R): This is because adolescent spends and interested in spending more time in social circle.

(a) (A) is true but (R) is false
(b) (A) is false but (R) is true
(c) Both (A) and (R) are true
(d) Both (A) and (R) are false

144. Match the diseases given in List I with affected organ in List II:

List I	**List II**
A. Neprosis	(i) Pancrease
B. Diabetes	(ii) Kidney
C. Arteriosclerosis	(iii) Intestine
D. Celiac Disease	(iv) Blood vessel
	(v) Heart

Codes:	A	B	C	D
(a)	(ii)	(i)	(v)	(iii)
(b)	(ii)	(i)	(iv)	(iii)
(c)	(iv)	(i)	(iii)	(ii)
(d)	(iii)	(i)	(ii)	(iv)

145. Match the following list of standardization marks from List I with products in List II:

List I	**List II**
A. Agmark	(i) Squash
B. FPO	(ii) Shawl
B. ISI	(iii) Honey
D. Wool mark	(iv) Biscuits

Codes:	A	B	C	D
(a)	(i)	(iv)	(iii)	(ii)
(b)	(ii)	(i)	(iv)	(iii)
(c)	(iv)	(i)	(iii)	(ii)
(d)	(iii)	(i)	(iv)	(ii)

Answer

143. (d) 144. (a) 145. (d)

146. The normal systolic and diastolic blood pressure for adult is:

(a) 140/100 mm/Hg (b) 120/80 mm/Hg
(c) 120/90 mm/Hg (d) 110/70 mm/Hg

147. Human resources are those which:

(a) are community facilities
(b) are material goods
(c) are inherent in persons
(d) include money

148. Match the deficiency diseases with their nutrients:

List I	List II
A. Kwashiorkor	(i) Thiamin
B. Pernicious Anemia	(ii) Riboflavin
C. Beri Beri	(iii) Folic Acid
D. Glossitis	(iv) Vitamin D
E. Osteoporosis	(v) Protein

Codes:	A	B	C	D	E
(a)	(i)	(iv)	(iii)	(ii)	(v)
(b)	(v)	(iii)	(i)	(ii)	(iv)
(c)	(iv)	(i)	(iii)	(ii)	(v)
(d)	(iii)	(i)	(ii)	(iv)	(v)

149. Match List I with List II:

List I	List II
A. Maslow	(i) Exosystem
B. Bronfenbrenner	(ii) Identity formation
C. Erikson	(iii) Zone of proximal development
D. Vygetsky	(iv) Hierarchy of Needs

Codes:	A	B	C	D
(a)	(i)	(iv)	(iii)	(ii)
(b)	(ii)	(i)	(iv)	(iii)

Answer

146. (b) 147. (c) 148. (b)

(c)	(iv)	(i)	(iii)	(ii)
(d)	(iv)	(i)	(ii)	(iii)

150. Give the correct sequence in which language is acquired during the early years:

(i) Holophrase (ii) Babbling
(iii) Telegraphic speech (iv) Expressive jargon

Codes:

(a)	(ii)	(iv)	(i)	(iii)
(b)	(ii)	(i)	(iv)	(iii)
(c)	(iv)	(i)	(ii)	(iii)
(d)	(iii)	(i)	(ii)	(iv)

151. **Assertion (A):** Disciplining methods adopted by parents influence the personality of the child.

Reason (R): Power Assertive method adopted by parents help raise calm and non-aggressive children.

(a) (A) is true but (R) is false
(b) (A) is false but (R) is true
(c) Both (A) and (R) are true
(d) Both (A) and (R) are false

152. Major source of energy for the body is:

(a) Protein (b) Glucose
(c) Fat (d) All of the above

153. Which of the following properties is not a primary property?

(a) Strength (b) Tenacity
(c) Flexibility (d) Density

154. Rh incompatibility occurs, when blood of:

(a) Mother is Rh +ve and fetus is Rh –ve
(b) Mother is Rh –ve and fetus is Rh +ve
(c) Mother is Rh –ve and fetus is Rh –ve
(d) Mother is Rh +ve and fetus is Rh +ve

Answer

149. (d) 150. (a) 151. (c) 152. (c) 153. (b)
154. (b)

155. Authoritarian child-rearing style:

(i) Harsh control (ii) Highly demanding
(iii) Lax control (iv) Understanding
(v) Firm control (vi) Non-responsive

Codes:

(a) (i), (iii) and (iv) are correct
(b) (iii), (ii) and (vi) are correct
(c) (vi), (v), (iii) and (ii) are correct
(d) (i), (ii) and (vi) are correct

156. **Assertion (A):** Certain amino acids which are termed essential are to be obtained from protein in the diet.

Reason (R): Since they are obtained from protein in the diet.

(a) (A) is true but (R) is false
(b) (A) is false but (R) is true
(c) Both (A) and (R) are true
(d) Both (A) and (R) are false

157. **Assertion (A):** People lose weight rapidly in the beginning when they start following weight reduction diet.

Reason (R): Glycogen stores are mobilized which is accompanied by loss of water.

(a) (A) is true but (R) is false
(b) (A) is false but (R) is true
(c) Both (A) and (R) are false
(d) Both (A) and (R) are true

158. Arrange in a correct sequence:

(i) Genital stage (ii) Anal stage
(iii) Latency stage (iv) Phallic stage

Codes:

(a) (ii), (iv), (iii), (i) (b) (iv), (ii), (i), (iii)
(c) (iii), (ii), (iv), (i) (d) (i), (iii), (ii), (iv)

Answer

155. (d) 156. (c) 157. (d) 158. (c)

159. Match an item with following lists:

List I	List II
A. Child care	(i) Oldage Homes
B. Geriatric care	(ii) Nursing Homes
C. Care of sick	(iii) Creche
D. Abandoned children	(iv) Hostel
	(v) Orphanage

Codes:	A	B	C	D
(a)	(iii)	(i)	(ii)	(v)
(b)	(ii)	(v)	(iv)	(iii)
(c)	(iv)	(i)	(v)	(ii)
(d)	(iii)	(i)	(ii)	(iv)

160. A common fear experienced during infancy is:
(a) Fear of strangers (b) Fear of darkness
(c) Fear of animals (d) Fear of ghosts

161. The process of rural development requires three services:
(a) Research, farmers and extension
(b) Home makers, teaching and extension
(c) Research, teaching and extension
(d) Guidance, research and training

162. Match the following:

List I	List II
A. Kratomalacia	(i) Symmetrical Dermatitis
B. Rickets	(ii) Moon Face
C. Pellagra	(iii) Pale skin
D. Kwashiorkor	(iv) Blindness
	(v) Pigeon Chest

Codes:	A	B	C	D
(a)	(iv)	(v)	(i)	(ii)
(b)	(ii)	(i)	(iv)	(iii)
(c)	(iv)	(i)	(iii)	(ii)
(d)	(iii)	(i)	(v)	(iv)

Answer

159. (a) 160. (a) 161. (c) 162. (a)

163. Give the right order of the acquisition of the cognitive structures from infancy to adolescence:

(i) Seriation (ii) Deferred imitation
(iii) Abstract thinking (iv) Animism

(a) (iv), (i), (ii), (iii) (b) (iv), (iii), (ii), (i)
(c) (iii), (ii), (i), (iv) (d) (iv), (i), (ii), (iii)

164. **Assertion (A):** Piaget's theory is concerned about quantities changes in intellectual development.

Reason (R): Piaget's theory studies changes in the structure of intelligence; how thinking gradually moves from sensorimotor to abstract reasoning through the span of childhood towards adulthood.

(a) (A) is true but (R) is false
(b) (A) is false but (R) is true
(c) Both (A) and (R) are true
(d) Both (A) and (R) are false

165. Erikson's stage of development of trust versus mistrust most closely matches Freud's:

(a) Genital stage (b) Differentiation stage
(c) Oral stage (d) Oedipal stage

166. To plot Histogram from frequency distribution the following are used on X-axis:

(a) Real limits of class intervals
(b) Apparent limits of class intervals
(c) Midpoints of class intervals
(d) Upper limits of class intervals

167. **Assertion (A):** Hypertension is a risk factor for CHD.

Reason (R): High blood pressure leads to raised cholesterol levels.

(a) (A) is true but (R) is false
(b) (A) is false but (R) is true

Answer

163. (d) 164. (c) 165. (c) 166. (a) 167. (b)

(c) Both (A) and (R) are true
(d) Both (A) and (R) are false

168. Write the correct sequence of Piaget's cognitive stages:
(i) Preoperational (ii) Sensorimotor
(iii) Concrete (iv) Formal

Codes:

(a) (iv), (i), (ii), (iii) (b) (iv), (iii), (ii), (i)
(c) (iii), (ii), (i), (iv) (d) (ii), (i), (iii), (iv)

169. RDA's for Indian women are based on reference women who has:
(a) Body weight 50 kg and height 1.40 m
(b) Body weight 55 kg and height 1.61 m
(c) Body weight 48 kg and height 1.56 m
(d) Body weight 52 kg and height 1.37 m

170. Sociometry is a tool to measure child's
(a) Intelligence level
(b) Behaviour problems
(c) Relationship with peers
(d) Relationship with parents

171. Language development in children is promoted through:
(i) Storytelling (ii) Conversation
(iii) Social participation (iv) Solitary play

Codes:

(a) (i) and (iii) are correct
(b) (ii) and (iii) are correct
(c) (i), (ii) and (iii) are correct
(d) (ii), (iii) and (iv) are correct

172. **Assertion (A):** Acute Renal failure means the kidneys have failed suddenly.

Reason (R): Various toxins or severe blood loss or trauma affect kidney functioning.

(a) (A) is true but (R) is false
(b) (A) is false but (R) is true

Answer

168. (d) 169. (b) 170. (c) 171. (c)

(c) Both (A) and (R) are true
(d) Both (A) and (R) are false

173. **Assertion (A):** Standing in a static posture is fatiguing.

Reason (R): Blood circulation is affected in the extremities while standing for work.

(a) (A) is true but (R) is false
(b) (A) is false but (R) is true
(c) Both (A) and (R) are true but (R) is not the complete explanation
(d) Both (A) and (R) are false

174. **Assertion (A):** Home is a place for development of both sexes through equal opportunities.

Reason (R): The personal and professional development of both sexes is not possible within home.

(a) (R) is true but (A) is false
(b) (R) is false but (A) is true
(c) Both (A) and (R) are true
(d) Both (A) and (R) are false

175. Arrange constituent processes of observational learning in correct sequence:

(i) Production (ii) Motivation
(iii) Retention (iv) Attention

Codes:

(a) (iv), (i), (ii), (iii)
(b) (iv), (iii), (i), (ii)
(c) (iii), (ii), (i), (iv)
(d) (iii), (iv), (ii), (i)

176. Level of Intelligent Quotient of educable mentally challenged child is:

(a) 0-25 (b) 50-75
(c) 25-50 (d) 75-100

Answer

172. (c) 173. (c) 174. (b) 175. (b) 176. (d)

177. Bending and carrying respectively belong to which kind of effort?

(a) Pedal and Mental (b) Torsal and Manual
(c) Manual and Pedal (d) Pedal and Torsal

178. The symptoms in kidney failure patients are:

(i) GFR 90 ml/min (ii) GFR 20 ml or less/min
(iii) Oliguria (iv) Polyuria
(v) Oedema

Codes:

(a) (iv), (ii) and (i) (b) (ii), (iii) and (v)
(c) (iv), (iii) and (i) (d) (iv), (v) and (ii)

179. Immunization is necessary for children:

(i) To develop defence mechanism in the body
(ii) To increase nutritional status
(iii) To reduce discomfort
(iv) To reduce incidence of viral and infectious diseases

Codes:

(a) (i) and (iii) are correct
(b) (i) and (iv) are correct
(c) (ii) and (iv) are correct
(d) (iii) and (iv) are correct

180. **Assertion (A):** Consistent sleep routines are advisable for all children right from birth.

Reason (R): It increases separation anxiety and deprives stimulation.

(a) (A) is true but (R) is false
(b) (A) is false but (R) is true
(c) Both (A) and (R) are true
(d) Both (A) and (R) are false

181. **Assertion (A):** Post-mature babies are generally long and thin as they receive insufficient blood supply towards the end of gestation.

Answer

177. (b) 178. (b) 179. (b) 180. (c)

Reason (R): The aged placenta is less efficient to supply oxygen.

(a) (A) is true but (R) is wrong explanation
(b) (A) is false but (R) is true
(c) Both (A) and (R) are true
(d) Both (A) and (R) are false

182. Arrange in the correct sequence, the symptoms of diabetes as they appear with advancement of disease:

(i) Dehydration (ii) Glycosuria
(iii) Polyurea (iv) Ketosis
(v) Hyperglycemia (vi) Diabetic coma

Codes:

(a) (i), (ii), (iii), (iv), (v), (vi)
(b) (iv), (i), (vi), (ii), (iii), (v)
(c) (iii), (iv), (i), (ii), (vi), (v)
(d) (v), (ii), (iii), (i), (iv), (vi)

183. Which mother is most likely to give birth to a down's syndrome baby?

(a) A mother who is tall, under weight, 25 years old, and who takes narcotics
(b) A mother who is 30 years old, overweight, and who drinks wine and smokes.
(c) A mother who is a jogger, in good health, 45 years old, and who neither smokes and nor drinks
(d) A mother who is Rh-negative, overweight, 20 years old, and who neither drinks or smokes

184. HDL is synthesized and secreted from:

(a) Kidneys (b) Puncreas
(c) Liver (d) Muscles

185. Releasing pent up emotional energy is:

(a) Body control (b) Emotional catharsis
(c) Mental Balance (d) Emotional Security

Answer

181. (a) 182. (d) 183. (b) 184. (c) 185. (b)

186. Dyslexic refers to individuals who have difficulty in:
(a) Learning to stand
(b) Learning to express
(c) Learning to speak
(d) Learning to read and write

187. Germ cells are formed by a process called:
(a) Meiosis (b) Mitosis
(c) Ovulation (d) Crossing over

188. Normal BMI for adult Asians as suggested by WHO is:
(a) 18-23 kg/m^2 (b) 19-24 kg/m^2
(c) 20-25 kg/m^2 (d) 21-26 kg/m^2

189. Generally visually impaired persons have visual acuity of:
(a) 2/200 (b) 20/100
(c) 20/70 (d) 20/200

190. The female sex hormone is:
(a) Androgen (b) Prolactin
(c) Estrogen (d) Oxytocin

191. Which of the following is a stationary knife?
(a) Band (b) Round
(c) Straight (d) Die

192. **Assertion (A):** A secondary circular reaction involves an action that has an effect on an object in the infant's environment.

Reason (R): Secondary circular reaction is the only process which involves symbolic play.
(a) (A) is true but (R) is false
(b) (A) is false but (R) is true
(c) Both (A) and (R) are true
(d) Both (A) and (R) are false

Answer

186. (d) 187. (a) 188. (a) 189. (d) 190. (c)
191. (a) 192. (b)

193. Arrange the correct sequence of cognitive process:
(i) Reflexes
(ii) Primary circular reactions
(iii) Secondary circular reactions
(iv) Mental combinations

Codes:

(a) (i), (ii), (iii), (iv) (b) (iv), (iii), (ii), (i)
(c) (iii), (ii), (i), (iv) (d) (iii), (iv), (ii), (i)

194. Match the diseases (List I) with their organs (List II):

List I	List II
A. Diabetes	(i) Liver
B. Celiac disease	(ii) Kidney
C. Nephritis	(iii) Gall bladder
D. Cholelithiasis	(iv) Pancrease
	(v) Intestines

Codes:	A	B	C	D
(a)	(iii)	(iv)	(i)	(ii)
(b)	(iv)	(v)	(ii)	(iii)
(c)	(iv)	(i)	(iii)	(v)
(d)	(iii)	(i)	(v)	(iv)

195. Match the following in List I with List II:

List I

A. Resources B. Human Resources
C. Economic Resources D. Non-Human Resources

List II

(i) Ability skill
(ii) Materials and human abilities
(iii) Tangible resources
(iv) Knowledge, time, community resources
(v) Resources and in production and distribution

Answer

193. (a) 194. (b) 195. (d)

Codes:	A	B	C	D
(a)	(iii)	(iv)	(i)	(ii)
(b)	(iv)	(iii)	(v)	(ii)
(c)	(iv)	(i)	(iii)	(ii)
(d)	(ii)	(i)	(v)	(iii)

196. **Assertion (A):** A kwashiorkor child shows oedema of the lower limbs.

Reason (R): The kidneys are not able to excrete sodium thus causing water retention.

(a) (A) is true but (R) is false
(b) (A) is false but (R) is true
(c) Both (A) and (R) are true
(d) Both (A) and (R) are false

197. Sleeves most appropriate for infants garment are:

(i) Leg of Mutton (ii) Saddler
(iii) Kimono (iv) Raglan

Find the right combination according to code:

(a) (ii) and (iii) are correct
(b) (iii) and (iv) are correct
(c) (i) and (ii) are correct
(d) (ii) and (iv) are correct

198. Speciousness in interiors can be achieved by:

(i) Using cool colour scheme
(ii) Using low furniture
(iii) Placing mirrors and glasses
(iv) More numbers of windows and doors

Codes:

(a) (ii), (iii) and (iv) are correct
(b) (iii) and (iv) are correct
(c) (i), (ii) and (iv) are correct
(d) (i), (ii) and (iii) are correct

Answer

196. (c) 197. (b) 198. (d) 199. (b)

199. **Assertion (A):** Celiac disease is an autoimmune inflammatory disease of small intestine.

Reason (R): It is precipitated by the ingestion of gluten.

(a) (A) is true but (R) is false
(b) (A) is false but (R) is true
(c) Both (A) and (R) are true
(d) Both (A) and (R) are false

Chapter 7

Non-formal, Extension Education and Communication

1. Duty of care means:
   (a) Accepting responsibility for other people's mistakes
   (b) Giving out advice and relevant accident forms to injured members
   (c) Having a working knowledge of rules
   (d) Accepting responsibility for health and safety in workplace
2. Treatment from stings is:
   (a) Put patient in a warm shower
   (b) Rub with sand to stop the burn
   (c) Wash with freshwater and apply ice
   (d) Wash with seawater and apply ice
3. What is the most correct procedure for first aid documentation?
   (a) Gather information from bystanders and record in patrol log book
   (b) Record events as witnessed, signed by first aider and kept on file
   (c) Check with patient as to cause of injury, ensure next of kin notified and verbally pass information onto ambulance/paramedics
   (d) Record all events as stated by bystanders and ensure patient signs as correct record

Answer

1. (d) 2. (d) 3. (b)

4. How is vertigo treated?
   (a) No treatment is required (b) Medication
   (c) Surgery (d) All of the above

5. What causes vertigo?
   (a) Insufficient rest (b) An inner-ear problem
   (c) Poor diet (d) Excessive weight

6. Symptoms of shock include:
   (a) Rapid, weak pulse (b) Confusion
   (c) Pale, cold clammy skin (d) Breathless and nausea

7. According to UN studies:
   (a) The vast majority of the world's young people have no idea how HIV is transmitted
   (b) The vast majority of the world's young people have no idea how to protect themselves
   (c) Adolescence is the time when the majority of people become sexually active and the tragic consequence is that they fall prey to HIV
   (d) (a), (b) and (c)

8. Checking for circulation involves:
   (a) Feeling for pulse
   (b) Feeling for pulse and observing patient's colour
   (c) Feeling for pulse, observing patient's colour and looking for signs of movement
   (d) Feeling for breathing

9. HIV/AIDS can be prevented through:
   (a) The use of good quality condom in every sexual intercourse
   (b) The use of protective gloves when handling blood or body fluids
   (c) Use of uncontaminated skin-piercing equipment
   (d) All of the above

Answer

4. (d) 5. (b) 6. (c) 7. (d) 8. (b)
9. (d)

10. What is inversion?
    (a) Lifting the medial border of the foot
    (b) Pointing the toe upwards
    (c) Pointing the toe downwards
    (d) Lifting the lateral border of the foot
11. Which of the following is caused by smoking?
    (a) Premature baldness in men
    (b) Chest hair on women
    (c) Cough with phlegm
    (d) Autism
12. What are the advantages of having a baby without medication?
    (a) Babies born without drugs are more active and alert
    (b) Right after birth the mother can comfort, stroke and gaze at her baby
    (c) Breast feeding is more easily established
    (d) All of the above
13. Why has "rooming-in" become normal at some hospitals?
    (a) This practice saves space in crowded hospitals.
    (b) Without the baby in the room mothers don't have anything to do
    (c) Researchers have learned that constant connection between mother and baby is very important
    (d) Due to hospital cutbacks, nurses don't have time to carry the babies back and forth from the nursery to their mothers
14. The peripheral nervous system is divided into 3 further systems. Which of the following is not one of these three systems?
    (a) Cranial nerves
    (b) Spinal nerves
    (c) Precentral nervous system
    (d) Autonomic nervous system

Answer

10. (a) 11. (c) 12. (d) 13. (c) 14. (c)

15. If an experimenter points to an unfamiliar object and says "that's foff", children will almost always guess that "foff" refers to:
    (a) Some part of the object
    (b) The whole object
    (c) The material from which the object is made
    (d) The colour of the object
16. What is efficiency in health care?
    (a) The allocation of resources between individuals and social groups
    (b) The allocation of resources to maximize health benefits
    (c) The allocation of resources to achieve the expected result
    (d) The allocation of resources to reduce cost
17. Two main mechanisms involved in neck injuries effecting surf lifesavers (aquatic injuries) are:
    (a) forward bending (flexion) and horizontal compression
    (b) vertical extension and backward bending (flexion)
    (c) vertical compression and forward bending (flexion)
    (d) vertical compression and backward bending (flexion)
18. When performing mouth to mask resuscitation, which is the preferred jaw lift?
    (a) Jaw support (b) Pistol grip
    (c) Jaw thrust (d) Either method
19. How would you treat a person who had a blister?
    (a) Pierce the sin to allow the fluid to drain out and then cover with a plaster
    (b) Apply surgical spirit to the area to harden the skin
    (c) Apply talc to dry the area out
    (d) Apply calamine lotion

Answer

15. (a) 16. (c) 17. (d) 18. (c) 19. (c)
19. (b)

20. Why do formula companies make formula?
    (a) To help the two mothers in one hundred who can't breast feed
    (b) To make it easier for other people to feed your baby
    (c) To support the dairy industry
    (d) To make money
21. Thermotherapy is a treatment using
    (a) ice (b) cold water
    (c) heat (d) wind
22. Smokers are how much more likely than non-smokers to develop the scaly, red, chronic skin condition called psoriasis?
    (a) 25% (b) 50%
    (c) Twice (d) 400 times
23. What is a symptom of liver disease?
    (a) Jaundice
    (b) When bile flow stops or decreases
    (c) An enlarged liver
    (d) All of the above
24. What is the best way to avoid the risk of prostate cancer?
    (a) Stay out of the sun
    (b) Take a calcium supplement daily
    (c) Eat a diet rich in fruits, vegetables and whole grains
    (d) Drink tomato juice every morning
25. Should all women take estrogen replacement therapy when they reach menopausal age?
    (a) Yes (b) No
    (c) Can't say (d) None of these
26. How does a pregnant woman know how to give birth?
    (a) Her body will do the right things automatically
    (b) Her doctor or midwife will tell her

Answer

20. (a) 21. (c) 22. (d) 23. (d) 24. (c)
25. (a)

(c) She can read any book on childbirth
(d) Friends and relatives can tell her

27. At what age is it recommended for a woman to have her first mammogram if she does not have a family history of breast cancer or is not considered at high risk?
(a) 30 (b) 35
(c) 40 (d) 45

28. At what age has a woman acquired 98% of her skeletal mass?
(a) 12 (b) 16
(c) 20 (d) 25

29. HIV/AIDS is:
(a) Creating orphans
(b) Leading to increased child labour
(c) Increasing drop out of schools
(d) All of the above

30. HIV/AIDS is transmitted by
(a) Kissing
(b) Hugging
(c) Shaking hands
(d) Unprotected sexual intercourse

31. HIV/AIDS is not transmitted by
(a) Blood transfusions
(b) Organ or tissue transplant
(c) Use of contaminated injection
(d) Sharing toilets or wasting facilities

32. HIV can
(a) Only enter the body through naturally moist places
(b) Penetrate unbroken skin
(c) Penetrate broken skin
(d) (a) and (c)

Answer

26. (a) 27. (b) 28. (c) 29. (d) 30. (d)
31. (d) 32. (d)

33. What workplaces can do to ensure that their HIV/AIDS programme tackle the problem of young people infected with HIV is by:
    (a) Reaching especially vulnerable young people, such as injecting drug users
    (b) Special messages delivered to young workers sensitively, with the right language and relevant to their age, by young people
    (c) Right education provided in the workplace for parent workers to teach their children, grandchildren, or younger siblings on how to protect themselves
    (d) All of the above

34. It's okay to let babies cry for long periods of time because:
    (a) It will clear their lungs
    (b) It probably won't produce enough cortisol to permanently damage the growing brain
    (c) It probably won't impair the child's sense of basic trust for the rest of his life
    (d) None of the above

35. Babies are given the ability to cry by nature. Why?
    (a) So that a baby can make life miserable for the parents
    (b) So that a baby's lungs will develop
    (c) So that a baby can feel important
    (d) So that a baby can signal others when it needs something

36. What things does a woman not need when she is giving birth?
    (a) A fast ride in a taxi
    (b) To feel that those around her are in a hurry for her to deliver her baby
    (c) To feel she is causing problems for those around her
    (d) All of the above are correct

Answer

33. (d) 34. (d) 35. (d) 36. (d)

37. Why is falling in love with your baby at the time of birth so important?
    (a) It makes the hard work of looking after a baby seem less like work
    (b) It feels good
    (c) The baby is happier
    (d) The baby will be born more quickly
38. When a baby is completely separated from its mother and other attachment figures, and does not receive responsive substitute mothering, what happens when the mother returns?
    (a) The baby won't recognize her after all that time
    (b) The baby ignores her in order to try to pay her back for leaving
    (c) The baby doesn't trust her and is afraid to get attached to her again
    (d) None of the above
39. What benefit is there in the development of babies who are worn in slings?
    (a) They have improved large and small muscle development
    (b) They develop faster in language
    (c) They have no problem in learning to crawl and walk
    (d) All of the above
40. If you decided to wear your baby you would find:
    (a) Lots of people who would think it is weird
    (b) Looking after your baby was a lot easier than you thought
    (c) You would develop a closer relationship with your baby
    (d) All of the above

Answer

37. (a) 38. (c) 39. (d) 40. (d)

41. Baby wearing for at least a few hours each day will:
    (a) Only spoil the baby
    (b) Help parents bond with their baby
    (c) Make the baby dizzy
    (d) All of the above
42. What situation would Dr. White suggest for parents to avoid sibling rivalry?
    (a) Have children who were born more than three years apart
    (b) Treat all of your children fairly and exactly the same way
    (c) Have only one child
    (d) Have a puppy that is not toilet trained for six months before having any children
43. Which of the following situations is an example of the defense mechanism called "rationalization"?
    (a) A person who gets drunk everyday, says he do not has a problem with alcohol
    (b) A person who fails in driver's exam says the examiner just didn't like him
    (c) When a wife asks her husband to talk about a problem they have been experiencing, he says that he has to go outside to water the lawn
    (d) All of the above
44. Why should we attempt to become familiar with the defense mechanisms that we ourselves use?
    (a) By increasing our awareness of defense mechanisms we can come to understand ourselves better and keep ourselves honest
    (b) By knowing our defense mechanisms well we can teach our children how to develop them
    (c) By knowing our defense mechanisms, we can use them to get ahead in business and social situations

Answer

41. (b) 42. (b) 43. (b)

(d) By knowing how we use defense mechanisms, we can become more skilled in using them

45. We now know a great deal about the brain because:
(a) Scientists are a lot smarter now
(b) There are more women scientists now than there used to be
(c) The MRI, the PET scan and tracers have been developed brain than we did one hundred years ago
(d) All of the above

46. At approximately what age does a child begin to develop a reciprocal relationship with his/her caretaker?
(a) From around 18-24 months
(b) 16-18 months
(c) 24-30 months
(d) None of the above

47. Anxiety disorders used to be classified as:
(a) Neuroses (b) Psychoses
(c) V mood disorders (d) Hysteria

48. Syntax refers to
(a) The meaning of words
(b) The sounds of words
(c) The rules by which words are combined
(d) The symbols used to designate words

49. The tendency to assume that there is a greater similarity among members of the out-groups than members of in-groups is called:
(a) Out-group homogeneity
(b) In-group homogeneity
(c) Out-group heterogeneity
(d) In-group heterogeneity

Answer

44. (a) 45. (c) 46. (a) 47. (a) 48. (c)
49. (a)

50. The biggest risk factor for sudden cardiac arrest death is:
    (a) High Blood Pressure smoking
    (b) Smoking
    (c) High blood cholesterol
    (d) Physical inactivity

51. A healthy person over 35 years of age should have their blood cholesterol checked
    (a) Every year (b) Every 2 years
    (c) Every 3 years (d) Every 4 years

52. Exercise burns
    (a) Protein (b) Calories
    (c) Nutrients (d) Vitamins

53. What percentage of women of childbearing age does premenstrual syndrome effect?
    (a) Less than 10% (b) 10-20% and 30-40%
    (c) 40-50% (d) More than 50%

54. Which of the following diseases is classified as an autoimmune disease?
    (a) Hypothyroidism (b) Rheumatoid Arthritis
    (c) Multiple Sclerosis (d) Psoriasis

55. The two most important dental health habits are:
    (a) Brushing twice daily and rinsing with mouthwash after each brushing
    (b) Brushing after every meal and using a water pick device daily
    (c) Brushing twice daily and flossing once a day
    (d) Flossing every day and rinsing with mouthwash after each floss

56. The reason we brush our teeth is:
    (a) to remove bacteria from tooth surfaces
    (b) to remove food particles from tooth surfaces

Answer

50. (a) 51. (a) 52. (b) 53. (b) 54. (b)
55. (a)

(c) both (a) and (b)
(d) neither (a) nor (b)

57. What hormone protects women against bone loss?
(a) Testosterone
(b) Estrogen
(c) Chemeosorogen
(d) All of these

58. Name three bones most often affected by osteoporosis
(a) Arm, shoulder and neck bones
(b) Hip, wrist and spinal bones
(c) Both (a) and (b)
(d) None of these

59. What is present in the body tissue of the brain, nervous system, liver and blood?
(a) Cholesterol
(b) Chromium
(c) Orotate
(d) None of these

60. The symptoms of gum disease are:
(a) a craving for sweets
(b) swollen gums that bleed easily
(c) yellowing teeth
(d) cavities

61. Untreated gum disease leads over time to what consequence?
(a) bad breath
(b) expensive dental bills
(c) tooth loss
(d) All of the above

62. Can a healthy lifestyle prevent Alzheimer's?
(a) Yes. Physicians say exercise, a low-fat diet, and ongoing mental stimulation can prevent the disease
(b) No. It's entirely genetic in origin
(c) Scientists aren't sure Alzheimer's can be prevented, but they say a healthy lifestyle may help protect brain cells
(d) None of these

Answer

56. (c) 57. (b) 58. (b) 59. (a) 60. (b)
61. (d) 62. (c)

63. Why do some moles change from flat to raised?
    (a) As the epidermis (outer skin layer) matures, the cells become thick and scaly
    (b) Scientists aren't sure
    (c) A minor mutation in our DNA code causes the cells to multiply
    (d) The flat mole becomes infected with cancerous cells and swells

64. What is a sneeze also called?
    (a) Reflexnutation (b) Sternutation
    (c) Inverse Reflex Action (d) Achoo

65. Addiction's most confounding symptom is:
    (a) a runny nose (b) violence
    (c) denial (d) a high fever

66. The most effective way to stop using drugs is:
    (a) Just say no
    (b) Undergo electroconvulsive shock therapy
    (c) Go to jail
    (d) Undergo drug rehabilitation treatment

67. Why do so many people have chronic diseases?
    (a) They don't eat a healthy diet
    (b) They don't take vitamins
    (c) It's a normal part of ageing
    (d) We're getting sick from the electromagnetic fields in our environment—the electric wires overhead, cell phones, microwave ovens, and stuff like that

68. Which item is not part of a home remedy for warts?
    (a) White glue (b) Nail polish
    (c) Banana peel (d) Potato skin

Answer

63. (a) 64. (b) 65. (c) 66. (d) 67. (a)
68. (a)

69. Congestive heart failure is:
    (a) A problem for 5 million Americans
    (b) B weakened heart that can't efficiently pump blood
    (c) Both (a) and (b)
    (d) The same thing as a heart attack
70. The typical person reporting back pain is:
    (a) African-American male, divorced and in his 50s
    (b) White female, married, in her 40s
    (c) Boys and girls, middle school, with heavy homework loads
    (d) Athletes, especially football and hockey players
71. Which of the following sentence is False?
    (a) As a rule of thumb more colour indicates greater antioxidant activity
    (b) Aiming for a variety of colours in a meal will, usually ensure a wider variety of nutrients
    (c) Phytochemical supplements are a good alternative to eating lots of fruits and vegetables
    (d) Lycopene may aid in prostate health. It is available in tomatoes
72. HIV/AIDS is:
    (a) One of the greatest challenges facing the world in the 21st century
    (b) An emergency of an unprecedented nature
    (c) A global disaster and threat to the world population
    (d) All of the above
73. Checking for circulation involves:
    (a) Feeling for pulse
    (b) Feeling for pulse and observing patient's colour
    (c) Feeling for pulse, observing patient's colour and looking for signs of movement
    (d) Feeling for breathing

Answer

69. (d) 70. (d) 71. (a) 72. (d) 73. (b)

74. Most deaths from heart attacks occur
    (a) In 1-2 hours after attack
    (b) In 15-30 minutes after attack
    (c) Within 24 hours of attack
    (d) Within an hour of attack

75. Conservation refers to—
    (a) The appreciation that certain properties of an object remain constant despite some perceptual changes in the object
    (b) The belief that the height of a column of liquid is the sole determinant of the liquid's total volume
    (c) The fact that the preoperational child is incapable of performing certain perceptual transformation in his head
    (d) The fact that preoperational children preserve thoughts about other people

76. "Extension education is formal and informal education." Who said this?
    (a) L.D. Kalsey (b) O.P. Dahama
    (c) D. Ensoninger (d) M.C. Burret

77. Soft water means:
    (a) Foaming with soap (b) Not foaming with soap
    (c) Rainwater (d) None of the above

78. BCG inoculation is done for—
    (a) Measles (b) Cholera
    (c) T.B. (d) Pneumonia

79. Delustering agent used in manmade fabric is:
    (a) Carbon tetrachloride
    (b) Titanium dioxide
    (c) Tri-chloro-benzene
    (d) Titanium-di-chloride

Answer

74. (d) 75. (a) 76. (b) 77. (c) 78. (c)
79. (b)

80. Total calories requirement for an average adult woman (sedentary) in a day?
    (a) 1790 (b) 2060
    (c) 1900 (d) 2880
81. Which is not a projective technique?
    (a) Model (b) Photograph
    (c) Flash card (d) Slides
82. Which does not come under community development?
    (a) State level (b) Country level
    (c) District level (d) Village level
83. Rearing and management of silk moth on large scale is known as:
    (a) Sericulture (b) Apiculture
    (c) Pisciculture (d) None of these
84. Who are most likely to develop gout?
    (a) Men older than 40 (b) Premenopausal women
    (c) Pregnant women (d) Boys starting puberty
85. Doping pure silicon with .... creates n-type silicon.
    (a) Phosphorus (b) Copper
    (c) Boron (d) None of these
86. The occurrence of varicose veins is more common in:
    (a) Men (b) Women
    (c) Teenage athletes (d) Bus drivers who sit all day
87. Which sentence is true?
    (a) About 25 per cent of Americans suffer from heartburn
    (b) Surgery is never used to treat heartburn patients
    (c) Heartburn is common among pregnant women
    (d) Heartburn cannot cause permanent damage
88. Besides drinking water we get water from what we eat and drink. What is not a good source of water?

Answer

80. (c) 81. (a) 82. (b) 83. (a) 84. (a)
85. (a) 86. (b) 87. (b)

(a) Scrambled eggs
(b) Broiled salmon
(c) Decaffeinated green tea
(d) Alcohol

89. How can you control mosquitoes to protect against dengue fever?
(a) Remove objects around your home that may collect rainwater
(b) Spray yourself with insecticide to prevent mosquito bites
(c) Quarantine people in your household for 72 hours
(d) Get rid of your pets

90. Where are taste buds for bitter taste situated?
(a) Front of tongue (b) Middle of tongue
(c) Back of tongue (d) All of the above

91. What is diabetes?
(a) A disease in which the pancreas produces a toxic form of insulin
(b) A disease in which the pancreas produces an insufficient amount of insulin or the body has a decreased ability to process insulin
(c) A disease brought on by an abnormal flow of insulin to the pancreas rather than the kidneys
(d) A disease in which the body abnormally rejects any form of sugar

92. What are the major forms of diabetes?
(a) Type 1, Type 2, obesity
(b) Type 1, Type 2, elderly
(c) Type 1, Type 2, gestational
(d) All of the above

93. Which sentence is false?
(a) Foot problems occur four times more often in women than in men

Answer

88. (d) 89. (b) 90. (c) 91. (b) 92. (c)

(b) The American Podiatric Medical Association recommends shopping for shoes in the morning, not the afternoon
(c) Neglect and improper foot care is the reason for most foot problems
(d) All of these

94. Which headache symptom may be a sign of a cerebral aneurysm (an abnormal ballooning of a portion of a blood vessel in the brain)?
(a) Worsening pain that includes nausea and vomiting and changes in speech or personality
(b) Sudden, violent pain
(c) Pain that is accompanied by fever and a stiff neck
(d) Pain that is aggravated by alcohol or sudden changes in temperature

95. Which occupation(s) carry a high risk factor of carpal tunnel syndrome?
(a) Typist (b) Meat packer
(c) Dentist (d) All of the above

96. How is the condition of carpal tunnel treated?
(a) Immobilizing the wrist
(b) Surgery
(c) Making lifestyle changes
(d) All of the above

97. Which of the following is not a hazard that can cause injury or harm in your place?
(a) Crowd control
(b) Spills and slippery surfaces like water, food and oil
(c) Incorrect storage including flammable materials having special storage requirements
(d) Environmental conditions such as sun exposure

Answer

93. (c) 94. (a) 95. (a) 96. (d) 97. (a)

98. What do warts look like?
    (a) Smooth, flat lesions the size of pinheads
    (b) Rough and round lumps that are lighter in colour than surrounding skin
    (c) Oval lumps that are darker than normal skin
    (d) All of the above

99. In a pattern dart can't be replaced by
    (a) Tucks (b) Dart tucks
    (c) Gathers (d) Control seam

100. The first step in extension programme planning is:
    (a) Framing objectives (b) Plan of action
    (c) Analysis of situation (d) Implementation

101. Swarnjayanti Gram Swarojgar Yojana was launched in the year:
    (a) 1993 (b) 1995
    (c) 1997 (d) 1999

102. Write the sequence of the given media of communication by the years they were started:
    (i) Television (ii) Radio
    (iii) Films (iv) Print

    Codes:
    (a) (iv), (iii), (ii), (i) (b) (i), (iii), (ii), (iv)
    (c) (ii), (i), (iii), (iv) (d) (ii), (iii), (i), (iv)

103. Match the communication medium from List I to category in List II:

List I	List II
A. Puppets	(i) Graphic aid
B. Charts	(ii) Electronic
C. Computer	(iii) Traditional media
D. Print	(iv) Mass media

Answer

98. (d) 99. (a) 100. (b) 101. (d) 102. (a)

Codes:	A	B	C	D
(a)	(i)	(iv)	(iii)	(ii)
(b)	(ii)	(i)	(iv)	(iii)
(c)	(iii)	(i)	(ii)	(iv)
(d)	(iii)	(ii)	(i)	(iv)

104. While washing fabrics of protein fibers colour bleeding can be prevented by using:
(a) Vinegar (b) Common salt
(c) Washing soda (d) Ammonia

105. The most distinguishing trait of autistic children is their:
(a) Echolalia
(b) Inadequate motor development
(c) Inability to relate to other people
(d) Low I.Q.

106. The purpose of using a poster is to:
(a) arouse interest (b) motivate
(c) create awareness (d) create understanding

107. Arrange the elements of communication to form a model:
(i) Message (ii) Audience
(iii) Source (iv) Channel

Codes:
(a) (i), (iv), (iii), (ii) (b) (i), (iii), (ii), (iv)
(c) (ii), (i), (iii), (iv) (d) (iii), (i), (iv), (ii)

108. Match the items in List I with List II:

List I	List II
A. Collective monologue	(i) Preschoolers
B. Divergent thinking	(ii) Problem-solving
C. Lanugo	(iii) Fetus body
D. Personal fable	(iv) Adolescence

Answer

103. (c) 104. (a) 105. (a) 106. (c) 107. (d)

Codes:	A	B	C	D
(a)	(iv)	(ii)	(iii)	(i)
(b)	(ii)	(i)	(iv)	(iii)
(c)	(i)	(ii)	(iv)	(iii)
(d)	(iii)	(i)	(ii)	(iv)

109. Current development extension programmes adopt:
   (a) Integrated approach
   (b) Participatory approach
   (c) Area development approach
   (d) Multinational approach

110. An effective extension programme:
   (a) Works as per the Government directives
   (b) Works as per the extension worker's plans
   (c) Takes care of the needs of the target group
   (d) Works within limited funds

111. Good communication happens only when
   (a) Messages are detailed and with illustrations
   (b) Right message is given in the right form and to right people
   (c) More messages are given to more people
   (d) Various media are used to give messages

112. **Assertion (A):** Effective communication is a combination of seeing, learning experiences complete.

   Reason (R): Exclusive use of AV aids makes, learning experiences complete.
   (a) (A) is true but (R) is false
   (b) (A) is false but (R) is true
   (c) Both (A) and (R) are true
   (d) Both (A) and (R) are false

113. **Assertion (A):** Posters used as audio visual aids compel attention and motivate action.

Answer

108. (a) 109. (a) 110. (c) 111. (b) 112. (a)

Reason (R): Posters help in communicating as they present abstract information in a graphic way.

(a) (A) is true but (R) is false
(b) (A) is false but (R) is true
(c) Both (A) and (R) are true
(d) Both (A) and (R) are false

114. Match the following List I with List II:

List I

A. Cross-sectional study B. Longitudinal study
C. Naturalistic study C. Experimental study

List II

(i) Observes children in naturally occurring situations
(ii) Observes same group(s) of children at different points of time
(iii) Observes children where circumstances are carefully controlled
(iv) Observes children of different ages at one point of time

Codes:	A	B	C	D
(a)	(i)	(iv)	(iii)	(ii)
(b)	(ii)	(i)	(iv)	(iii)
(c)	(iv)	(ii)	(i)	(iii)
(d)	(iii)	(i)	(ii)	(iv)

115. A method of service where food is displayed and the guests have to help themselves is termed as:

(a) Banquet (b) Buffet
(c) Counter service (d) Cafeteria service

116. According to Freud, a person could only become a mature, healthy adult if:

(a) Qualitative changes occurred in development
(b) Emotional conflicts were resolved

Answer

113. (a) 114. (c) 115. (b)

(c) Child had both parents
(d) Child received opportunities for physical growth

117. The concept of object permanence asserts:
(a) The object when disappears would appear if retrieved
(b) Mother's presence asserts object permanence
(c) The linguistic ability of the preschooler
(d) That objects continue to exist even though they may be out of sight

118. The four main principles of Extension Education are given by:
(a) Mildred Horton (b) Ruskin
(c) John Dewey (d) J. Paul Leagans

119. The Pilot Project which played an important role in rural development and planning was:
(a) Community Development Project
(b) Etawah Project
(c) National Extension Service Project
(d) Intensive Agriculture Development Project

120. The main basic functions of communication are:
(a) Six (b) Four
(c) Three (d) Five

121. To be a good communicator, the thumb rule is:
(a) To go to the community and listen to the people
(b) To go and start working
(c) To go and start talking with the people
(d) To go and show them some visuals

122. The following measure of Central Tendency and Dispersion are used in ANOVA:
(a) Mean and Standard Deviation
(b) Mean and Variance

Answer

116. (d) 117. (d) 118. (d) 119. (b) 120. (a)
121. (a)

(c) Mean and Standard Error
(d) Median and Standard Deviation

123. Match the following institution (List I) with the appropriate delivery system (List II):

List I	List II
A. Hospital	(i) Table service
B. Cafeteria	(ii) Counter service
C. Hotel	(iii) Pantry service
D. Hostel	(iv) Banquet
E. Railways	(v) Centralized

Codes:	A	B	C	D	E
(a)	(i)	(iv)	(iii)	(ii)	(v)
(b)	(ii)	(i)	(iv)	(iii)	(v)
(c)	(v)	(ii)	(iv)	(i)	(iii)
(d)	(iii)	(i)	(ii)	(iv)	(v)

124. Match the List I with List II:

List I	List II
A. Folder	(i) Single sheet of small size paper
B. Journals	(ii) Single printed sheet of big size paper
C. Leaflet	(iii) Containing research information
D. Bulletin	(iv) Printed bound booklet

Codes:	A	B	C	D
(a)	(ii)	(iii)	(i)	(iv)
(b)	(ii)	(i)	(iv)	(iii)
(c)	(iv)	(i)	(iii)	(ii)
(d)	(iii)	(i)	(ii)	(iv)

125. Some Adult Education Programmes are given below. Identify the correct order as per year of implementation:

(i) National Adult Education Programme
(ii) The gram sikshan mohim

Answer

122. (b) 123. (c) 124. (a)

(iii) Non-formal education for youth
(iv) Farmers' functional literacy projects

Codes:

(a)	(i)	(iv)	(iii)	(ii)
(b)	(ii)	(i)	(iv)	(iii)
(c)	(iv)	(i)	(ii)	(iii)
(d)	(ii)	(iv)	(iii)	(i)

126. There are six basic steps of extension teaching which are given below; arrange them in sequence:

(i) Desire (ii) Conviction
(iii) Interest (iv) Attention
(v) Action (vi) Satisfaction

Codes:

(a)	(iv)	(iii)	(i)	(ii)	(v)	(vi)
(b)	(ii)	(i)	(iv)	(iii)	(vi)	(v)
(c)	(iv)	(i)	(ii)	(iii)	(v)	(vi)
(d)	(iii)	(i)	(ii)	(iv)	(vi)	(v)

127. **Assertion (A):** Community Development Programme was started after Independence.

Reason (R): Community Development Programme aims at self-reliant and rural development.

(a) (A) is true but (R) is false
(b) (A) is false but (R) is true
(c) Both (A) and (R) are true
(d) Both (A) and (R) are false

128. **Assertion (A):** The involvement of youth, children and women in the development programme is a must for success.

Reason (R): Generally development programmes are designed for children, youth and women.

Answer

125. (d) 126. (a) 127. (b)

(a) (A) is true but (R) is false
(b) (A) is false but (R) is true
(c) Both (A) and (R) are true but (R) is not the correct answer
(d) Both (A) and (R) are false

129. Extension education as a discipline of teaching programme started in early:

(a) 1940s (b) 1950s
(c) 1960s (d) 1970s

130. The term Extension Education was first used in 1873 by the:

(a) Cambridge University
(b) Oxford University
(c) Banaras Hindu University
(d) University of Madras

131. Extension learner learn the ideas and practices by:

(i) Doing (ii) Reading
(iii) Watching (iv) Neighbour

Codes:

(a) (i), (ii) and (iii) are correct
(b) (i), (iii) and (iv) are correct
(c) (i) and (ii) are correct
(d) (i) and (iii) are correct

132. Innovative learner prefer specific teaching style:

(i) Discussion (ii) Question and Answer
(iii) Independent Project (iv) Audio Listening

Codes:

(a) (i), (ii) and (iii) are correct
(b) (ii), (iii) and (iv) are correct
(c) (i) and (ii) are correct
(d) (ii) and (iii) are correct

Answer

128. (c) 129. (c) 130. (a) 131. (c) 132. (c)

133. Which one of the following pairs is not correctly matched:
   (a) The observational method is the most commonly used method to study—behaviour of individuals
   (b) Questionnaire can either be—structured or unstructured
   (c) Thematic apperception test is used to draw inferences about—respondent's personality structure
   (d) Sociometry is a technique to study—emotional intelligence of children

134. **Assertion (A):** 'Time out' is a form of punishment in which children are removed from the immediate setting until they are ready to act appropriately.

   Reason (R): It is not a useful technique enough time for children to change their behaviour.
   (a) (A) is true but (R) is false
   (b) (A) is false but (R) is true
   (c) Both (A) and (R) are true
   (d) Both (A) and (R) are false

135. **Assertion (A):** NREGA recently named as (MGNREGA) Mahatma Gandhi National Rural Employment Guarantee Act on 2nd October 2006.

   Reason (R): This is largest public employment guarantee programme of rural area which ultimately aims at better livelihood security of villagers.
   (a) (A) is true but (R) is false
   (b) (A) is false but (R) is true
   (c) Both (A) and (R) are true and (R) is the correct explanation
   (d) Both (A) and (R) are true but (R) is not the correct explanation

136. Write the correct sequence of Indigenous model:
   (i) Community
   (ii) Local problems

Answer

133. (d) 134. (c) 135. (c)

(iii) Indigenous knowledge system
(iv) Solution by experts using local material

Codes:

(a) (iv), (i), (ii), (iii) (b) (i), (ii), (iii), (iv)
(c) (iii), (ii), (i), (iv) (d) (iii), (iv), (ii), (i)

137. Write the correct sequence of following media as per their appearance in India:

(i) Print (ii) Television
(iii) Radio (iv) Cinema

Codes:

(a) (iv), (i), (ii), (iii) (b) (iv), (iii), (ii), (i)
(c) (iii), (ii), (i), (iv) (d) (i), (iv), (iii), (ii)

138. Match the following:

List I

A. Behaviourism began with the work
B. Viewed the child as tabula rasa
C. Founder of child study movement
D. Viewed the child as developing within a complex system of relationship

List II

(i) G. Stanley Hall (ii) U. Bronfenbrenner
(iii) John Locke (iv) John Watson

Codes:	A	B	C	D
(a)	(iii)	(iv)	(i)	(ii)
(b)	(ii)	(i)	(iv)	(iii)
(c)	(iv)	(i)	(iii)	(ii)
(d)	(iv)	(iii)	(i)	(ii)

139. Match the List I with List II:

List I

A. Hindu Marriage Act
B. Medical Termination of Pregnancy

Answer

136. (b) 137. (d) 138. (d)

C. Dowry Prohibition Act
D. Protection of Women from Domestic Violence Act

List II

(i) 1955 (ii) 2005
(iii) 1971 (iv) 1961

Codes:	A	B	C	D
(a)	(i)	(iii)	(iv)	(ii)
(b)	(ii)	(i)	(iv)	(iii)
(c)	(iv)	(i)	(iii)	(ii)
(d)	(iii)	(i)	(ii)	(iv)

140. Match the List I with List II:

List I

A. Textbook of Mass Communication and Media
B. Extension Education and Communication
C. Participatory Rural Approval
D. Education and Communication for Development

List II

(i) Neela Mukherjee
(ii) O.P. Dharma and O.P. Bhatnagar
(iii) Uma Joshi
(iv) V.K. Dubey and Indira Bishnoi

Codes:	A	B	C	D
(a)	(iv)	(iii)	(i)	(ii)
(b)	(iii)	(iv)	(i)	(ii)
(c)	(iv)	(i)	(iii)	(ii)
(d)	(iii)	(i)	(ii)	(iv)

141. The study of basic sounds which constitute any language form is called:

(a) Phonology (b) Morphology
(c) Pragmatics (d) Semantics

Answer

139. (a) 140. (b) 141. (a)

142. Extension education is a:
   (a) Two-way channel   (b) Three-way channel
   (c) One-way channel   (d) Four-way channel

143. A single printed sheet of paper of small size, containing preliminary information relating to a topic is known as:
   (a) News-letter   (b) Bulletin
   (c) Leaflet   (d) Folder

144. An electronic audio-visual medium which provides pictures with synchronized sound is known as:
   (a) Television   (b) Film show
   (c) Drama   (d) Farm telecasts

145. Match List I with List II:

   List I

   A. Participatory approach   B. Adoption
   C. Tenth five-year plan   D. Culture

   List II

   (i) Following Practices
   (ii) 2002-2007
   (iii) Direct participation of people
   (iv) A learnt behaviour

Codes:	**A**	**B**	**C**	**D**
(a)	(iii)	(iv)	(i)	(ii)
(b)	(ii)	(i)	(iv)	(iii)
(c)	(iv)	(i)	(iii)	(ii)
(d)	(iii)	(i)	(ii)	(iv)

146. Aristotle model of communication has the following ingredients, arrange them in order of priority:
   (i) Speaker   (ii) Audience
   (iii) Speech

Answer

142. (a)   143. (c)   144. (c)   145. (d)

Codes:

(a) (iii), (i), (ii) (b) (i), (iii), (ii)
(c) (iii), (ii), (i) (d) (iii), (i), (ii)

147. Which of the following statements is an example of a casual statement:
   (a) Both boys and girls participate in sports activities
   (b) The incidence of childhood diseases decreases as the adolescent years approach
   (c) Young children may talk out loud without realizing it
   (d) When a woman in the first trimester of pregnancy contracts rubella, she may give birth to a deaf and blind baby

148. Non-formal education should be:
   (a) Democratic
   (b) Abstract and theoretical
   (c) Environment friendly
   (d) Teacher oriented

149. According to Lee Thayer (1968) the categories of the function of communication are:
   (a) six (b) four
   (c) three (d) five

150. Extension education as a discipline has its historical roots in:
   (a) India (b) U.S.A.
   (c) U.K. (d) Australia

151. Educational movies are generally long:
   (a) 10 mm (b) 7 mm
   (c) 16 mm (d) 15 mm

152. **Assertion (A):** All types of puppets used for educational purposes should be of prominent colour and appropriate size.

Answer

146. (b) 147. (d) 148. (d) 149. (a) 150. (b)
151. (c)

Reason (R): Being attractive puppets motivate learners.

(a) (A) is true but (R) is false
(b) (A) is false but (R) is true
(c) Both (A) and (R) are true
(d) Both (A) and (R) are false

153. Write the steps of extension educational process in sequence:

(i) Objectives (ii) Teaching
(iii) Evaluation (iv) Situation
(v) Reconsideration

Codes:

(a) (iv), (i), (ii), (v), (iii)
(b) (iv), (iii), (ii), (i), (v)
(c) (iii), (ii), (i), (iv), (v)
(d) (iii), (iv), (ii), (i), (v)

154. Arrange them in descending order of retaining from various teaching aids:

(i) Reading
(ii) Listening
(iii) Watching a film
(iv) Looking at charts/diagrams

Codes:

(a) (iv), (i), (ii), (iii) (b) (iv), (iii), (ii), (i)
(c) (iii), (i), (ii), (iv) (d) (iii), (ii), (i), (iv)

155. Match the following food service units in List I with types of service in List II:

List I	List II
A. Airlines	(i) Decentralized
B. Hostel	(ii) Counter
C. Hospital	(iii) Portable
D. Cafeteria	(iv) Scramble

Answer

152. (c) 153. (a) 154. (d)

E. Fast food unit (v) Waiter

(vi) Drive in

Codes:	A	B	C	D	E
(a)	(iii)	(iv)	(i)	(ii)	(vi)
(b)	(i)	(iii)	(v)	(iv)	(ii)
(c)	(iv)	(i)	(iii)	(ii)	(v)
(d)	(iii)	(i)	(ii)	(iv)	(vi)

156. This consists of two lists of statement regarding educational aids. Match the List I with List II:

List I	List II
A. Flannel Board	(i) Big, bold and simple
B. Illustration	(ii) Plywood, hardwood or cardboard
C. Lettering	(iii) Large, bold and printed
D. Colours	(iv) Few and pleasing

Codes:	A	B	C	D
(a)	(iii)	(iv)	(i)	(ii)
(b)	(ii)	(i)	(iv)	(iii)
(c)	(iv)	(i)	(iii)	(ii)
(d)	(i)	(ii)	(iv)	(iii)

157. Principle of operation of an electric water heater is by:

(a) Convection (b) Radiation

(c) Conduction (d) Induction

158. DRDA is functioning at

(a) District level (b) Block level

(c) Village level (d) State level

159. The sequential order of Extension Educational Process is:

(i) Objectives (i) Teaching

(iii) Situation (iv) Reconsideration

(v) Evluation

Answer

155. (b) 156. (d) 157. (d) 158. (a)

Codes:

(a) (iv), (i), (ii), (iii), (v) (b) (iv), (iii), (ii), (i), (v)
(c) (iii), (ii), (i), (iv), (v) (d) (iii), (i), (ii), (v), (iv)

160. Channels for participatory communication are:

(i) Community Radio (ii) Participatory Video
(iii) Street theatre (iv) Films

Codes:

(a) (i), (ii) and (iii) (b) (ii), (i) and (iii)
(c) (iii), (i) and (ii) (d) (i), (iii) and (iv)

161. **Assertion (A):** Communication whether interpersonal or between social systems involves interface, the common boundary of two systems.

Reason (R): The interface between families and other systems remain the same irrespective of their income.

(a) Both (A) and (R) is false
(b) (A) is false but (R) is true
(c) Both (A) and (R) are true
(d) (A) is true and (R) is false

162. **Assertion (A):** Mass communication is not appropriate for participatory communication.

Reason (R): Mass communication is largely monologue.

(a) (A) is true but (R) is false
(b) (A) is false but (R) is true
(c) Both (A) and (R) are true
(d) Both (A) and (R) are false

163. **Assertion (A):** A good communicator is a good listener.

Reason (R): Communication is a cyclic process.

(a) (A) is true but (R) is false
(b) (A) is false but (R) is true
(c) Both (A) and (R) are false
(d) Both (A) and (R) are true

Answer

159. (d) 160. (a) 161. (d) 162. (c) 163. (d)

164. The insulating material used in refrigerator these days is:
    (a) Fiber glass (b) Mica
    (c) Asbestos sheet (d) Polyurethane foam

165. Non-formal education programme can be organized wherever:
    (a) Classrooms are available
    (b) Teachers are available
    (c) Most convenient to learners
    (d) Classrooms and teachers both are available

166. The curriculum of non-formal education should be:
    (a) Formally approved
    (b) Flexible
    (c) Need specific of learner
    (d) Culturally based

167. The three-dimensional recognisable limitation of an object is known as:
    (a) Film (b) Specimen
    (c) Mock-ups (d) Poster

168. Deliberate manipulation of people's belief, values and behaviour through words, gestures, images is known as:
    (a) Publicity (b) Propaganda
    (c) Persuasion (d) Perception

169. The standards for space to be provided all around a building is referred to as:
    (a) Open space (b) Set back
    (c) Ventilation (d) Landscape

170. The type of communication best suited to address an audience is:
    (a) Mass communication
    (b) Group communication

Answer

164. (d) 165. (d) 166. (b) 167. (a) 168. (b)
169. (c)

(c) Interpersonal communication
(d) Cosmopolite communication

171. Expansion of IEC is:
(a) Information, Electronic and Communication
(b) International Export Council
(c) Information, Education and Communication
(d) Indian Economic Council

172. Which among these can be used for demonstration purposes?
(a) Flat pictures (b) Exhibit
(c) Flannel Boards (d) Displays

173. Extension work originated in various countries in different ways depending on local conditions as reported by:
(a) F.A.O. (b) W.H.O.
(c) Planning Commission (d) I.C.A.R.

174. Problem-solving cycle in extension is given by:
(a) Dewey (b) Russel
(c) Ensminger (d) Swanson and Claar

175. **Assertion (A):** With increase in family income the proportionate expenditure on food will increase.

Reason (R): As family income increases the family will be spending more money on food.
(a) (A) is true but (R) is false
(b) (A) is false but (R) is true
(c) Both (A) and (R) are true
(d) Both (A) and (R) are false

176. **Assertion (A):** Integrated Rural Development Programme ensure that beneficiaries have an opportunity to earn.

Reasoning (R): Any women oriented programme improves nutritional, educational and financial status of the family.

Answer

170. (a) 171. (c) 172. (d) 173. (c) 174. (a)
175. (c)

(a) (A) is true but (R) is false
(b) (A) is false but (R) is true
(c) Both (A) and (R) are false
(d) Both (A) and (R) are true

177. Give the correct sequence of the purchasing schedule:
(i) Select the market
(ii) Develop purchase order
(iii) Identify needs
(iv) Receive and inspect deliveries
(v) Write specification

Codes:

(a) (ii), (i), (v), (iii), (iv) (b) (v), (iii), (ii), (i), (iv)
(c) (iii), (ii), (i), (iv), (v) (d) (iii), (v), (ii), (i), (iv)

178. Arrange class of change in correct sequence as given by Mundel:
(i) Change in raw material
(ii) Change in production sequence
(iii) Change in body position and number and type of motions
(iv) Change in finished product
(v) Change in working arrangement and equipment

Codes:

(a) (ii), (i), (v), (iii), (iv) (b) (iii), (v), (ii), (iv), (i)
(c) (iii), (ii), (i), (iv), (v) (d) (iii), (iv), (ii), (i), (v)

179. Write the steps given Wilson and Gallup (1954) of Home Science extension teaching in a sequence:
(i) Interest (ii) Conviction
(iii) Attention (iv) Action
(v) Desire (vi) Satisfaction

Codes:

(a) (i), (ii), (iii), (iv), (v), (vi)
(b) (iii), (i), (v), (ii), (iv), (vi)

Answer

176. (d) 177. (d) 178. (b)

(c) (iii), (iv), (i), (ii), (vi), (v)
(d) (i), (iii), (ii), (iv), (v), (vi)

180. Write the elements of communication process in correct sequence:

(i) Channel
(ii) Treatment
(iii) Sender
(iv) Message
(v) Receiver

Codes:

(a) (ii), (i), (v), (iii), (iv)
(b) (iv), (iii), (ii), (i), (v)
(c) (iii), (iv), (ii), (i), (v)
(d) (iii), (iv), (ii), (i), (v)

181. Match the following Equipment in List I with food items which use them in List II:

List I	List II
A. Bainmaric	(i) Mutton curry
B. Salamander	(ii) Chapati
C. Steam cooker	(iii) Pizza
D. Food processor	(iv) Rice
E. Griddles	(v) Vegetable
	(vi) Ice cream

Codes:	A	B	C	D	E
(a)	(i)	(iii)	(iv)	(v)	(ii)
(b)	(ii)	(i)	(iv)	(iii)	(v)
(c)	(iv)	(i)	(iii)	(v)	(ii)
(d)	(iii)	(i)	(ii)	(iv)	(v)

182. **Assertion (A):** One of the best styles of parental discipline is democratic pattern.

Reason (R): Both parent and the child discuss and take decision.

(a) (A) is true but (R) is false
(b) (A) is false but (R) is true

Answer

179. (b) 180. (c) 181. (a)

(c) Both (A) and (R) are true
(d) Both (A) and (R) are false

183. **Assertion (A):** The effectiveness of audio visuals rely upon the skill of the user.

Reason (R): The AV aids are selected on the basis of the criteria used for teaching and learning.

(a) (A) is true but (R) is partially true
(b) (A) is false but (R) is true
(c) Both (A) and (R) are true
(d) Both (A) and (R) are false

184. Give the right sequence of Home Management Process:

(i) Energising (ii) Evaluation
(iii) Planning (iv) Adjusting
(v) Checking

Codes:

(a) (ii), (i), (v), (iii), (iv)
(b) (iv), (iii), (ii), (i), (v)
(c) (iii), (i), (v), (iv), (ii)
(d) (iii), (iv), (ii), (i), (v)

185. The sequential order of communication is:

(i) Message (ii) Sender
(iii) Decoder (iv) Encoder
(v) Receiver

Codes:

(a) (ii), (i), (v), (iii), (iv)
(b) (iv), (iii), (ii), (i), (v)
(c) (iii), (ii), (i), (iv), (v)
(d) (ii), (i), (iv), (iii), (v)

Answer

182. (c) 183. (a) 184. (c) 185. (d)

186. Match the following items:

List I

A. CD ROM
B. Video Conferencing
C. Satellite technology
D. Mime and Puppetry

List II

(i) Interactive Multimedia
(ii) Folk media
(iii) Computer stored media
(iv) Global Networking media

Codes:	**A**	**B**	**C**	**D**
(a)	(iii)	(i)	(iv)	(ii)
(b)	(ii)	(i)	(iv)	(iii)
(c)	(iv)	(i)	(iii)	(ii)
(d)	(iii)	(i)	(ii)	(iv)

187. Which two approaches are good in communicating messages to the community?

(i) Participatory approach
(ii) Training and visit approach
(iii) Commodity specialized approach
(iv) Direct approach by the community

Codes:

(a) (ii), (iii) and (iv)
(b) (ii) and (iv)
(c) (i), (iii) and (iv)
(d) (i), (ii) and (iii)

188. **Assertion (A):** The Swarnjayanti Gram Swarojgar Yojna was launched in April 1999 and is the only self-employment programme currently being implemented.

Reason (R): It aims at promoting micro-enterprises and to bring the poor families above the poverty line.

(a) (A) is true but (R) is false
(b) (A) is false but (R) is true

Answer

186. (a) 187. (d)

(c) Both (A) and (R) are true but (R) is not the correct explanation of (A)
(d) Both (A) and (R) are true and (A) is not the correct explanation of (R)

189. **Assertion (A):** Right to Education act which was implemented on 1st April, 2010 by Govt. of India.

Reason (R): It ensures education to all children of the country between the age of 6 years to 14 years.

(a) (A) is true but (R) is false
(b) (A) is false but (R) is true
(c) Both (A) and (R) are true but (A) is not the correct explanation of (R)
(d) Both (A) and (R) are true and (R) is not the correct explanation of (A)

190. Non-formal education is:

(i) An organized
(ii) Systematic
(iii) Highly institutionalised
(iv) An educational activity

Codes:

(a) (i), (ii) and (iv) are correct
(b) (ii) and (iii) are correct
(c) (i), (ii) and (iii) are correct
(d) (ii), (iii) and (iv) are correct

191. Which of the following are visual aids?

(i) Black Board (ii) Posters
(iii) Public address system (iv) Flash cards

Codes:

(a) (i) and (iii) are correct
(b) (i), (ii) and (iv) are correct

Answer

188. (c) 189. (d) 190. (a)

(c) (i), (ii) and (iii) are correct
(d) (ii), (iii) and (iv) are correct

192. **Assertion (A):** Home Management is not an all encompassing concept compared to decision-making or problem-solving.

Reason (R): Home Management does not consider the totality of managerial functioning.

(a) (A) is true but (R) is false
(b) (A) is false but (R) is true
(c) Both (A) and (R) are true
(d) Both (A) and (R) are false

Answer

191. (b) 192. (d)